YOU'LL BE A GREAT DADDY!

The Dad-To-Be Handbook

Jimmy Smeaux

I do not teach you anything. I just help you to know yourself.

—BRUCE LEE

To my Baby Doll – you'll always be my silly little Booger Face.
And to Chi-Chi – I'll never stop calling you my sweet baby Shlargins.

I wish you both unending happiness, and I'll always be by your side.

Printed in the United States of America

First Printing: October 2018
Jefferson & Jefferies

ISBN– 9781726704670

CONTENTS

INTRODUCTION

Having children changed me in ways I never could have imagined. I'm definitely not as big of a jackass as I used to be, and I'm much more thoughtful... that's for sure. But, it runs a lot deeper than that. I'm selfless now where I used to be fairly selfish. I'm accepting instead of judgmental. Everything I look at has a story behind it and everyone I meet leaves a bit of themselves in my heart somehow. Internally, I changed quite a bit when I first became a dad. I don't know... maybe I'm just getting soft in my old age. Either way, in my biased opinion, being a father is the greatest thing ever. Nothing else even comes close. I never realized I could love something so much. The love I feel toward my children is different than anything else I've experienced in my life. It's timeless, boundless, infinite and unmeasurable love, and it runs deeper than my soul. When my daughters come running up to the door every day after I get home from work, my heart absolutely melts. It never gets old. There's nothing I enjoy more in this world than seeing my daughters smile and laugh. If I sound overly-dramatic to you... just wait. You'll find out.

Let's cut right to the chase. You probably already want to ask me, "How do I make my child happy all the time while simultaneously preparing them for the future?" That's a great question, but it's not my question to answer.

My job is to prepare *you* to answer that question. That's what parenting is all about. I once had a boss delegate me a daily routine at work and she said, "Don't ever try to improve this process. Just follow the documentation exactly." That is quite possibly the worst advice anyone's ever given me. Please don't think like that. Please don't parent like that either. My processes are never written in stone. I change the way I approach parenting every day.

I want you to use my experience as something to build upon. I intentionally stay away from presenting a lot of specifics in this book because of that fact. At this point, you might even think you want specifics, but eventually you'll want to pave your own path. I want to give you the tools to help do just that.

Now, being a parent isn't scary, but thinking about being a parent can be frightening if you let it be. I know why it's scary. The thought of someone else depending on you and the level of responsibility involved in raising a child can be colossal weights on your shoulders at first. No, it's not easy to be a parent, but I doubt you'll ever care about it being easy. Odds are you'll only care about doing it right.

In my experience, the hardest part about parenting is the beginning – before you know what to expect, before you have all the answers, and before you're wise enough to admit you will never have all the answers. That's what this book is about – easing your fears of the unknown. I want to help you understand what's coming. I want you to be comfortable with what to expect. And, I hope to convince you of what not to expect as well. Some of what I talk about might sound overwhelming at first, but the more honest and accurate my descriptions are, the more at ease you'll feel in the end with what's to come.

My hope is that you'll sleep easier after reading this book. None of what I say will make you a great father. Some of what you'll find in this book should definitely help, but being a great father will always come from within. Actually, deep inside yourself, you already possess the qualities that will make you a great father. You might not believe that yet, but it's true. If you weren't already on the path toward being a great father, you wouldn't be reading this right now. The fire inside you is what will guide you the most throughout your parenting endeavors.

The unsettling feeling you have stirring in your stomach – the worry, fear, and anxiety – is actually a great sign. I used to play hockey when I was younger and I'd always get really nervous before games. Sometimes, I'd even become so nervous I'd get sick. I hated that feeling and I never fully understood it until one of my teammates gave me a great piece of advice. He said, "That's the feeling of intensity. It means you care. When you stop feeling nervous before games, it's time to quit hockey."

The intensity you feel right now is what will make you great. We'll come back to that point later. For now, I'll tell you a little bit more about how I view parenting.

CHAPTER 1 – PARENTING

I'm not going to tell you how to parent your kid. I believe one of the first unavoidable frustrations you'll come across will be to filter through other people's misguided opinions and unwarranted advice. I wouldn't be good at parenting your kid anyway. I'm not sure I'm all that great at parenting my own kids half the time. I'm only here to tell you what to expect. At times, I'll reference my own stories and parenting techniques as examples, but I'd always encourage you to err on the side of following your instinct (especially when in doubt). None of what I say in this book is meant to be preachy, absolute, or judgmental. You don't even need to agree with me all the time. Be skeptical of what I say. Judge my parenting techniques when I draw on personal happenings. Everything I write is meant to engage you, prepare you, and get you thinking about how *you* want to parent your kid. I know you won't do things the same way I did. That is actually a great sign – if you're analyzing where your parental opinions might differ from my own. You're well on your way!

Me... I'm just like you, only more self-conscious, worse looking, and less confident. We're a lot alike in that we're two completely different people with different perspectives, opinions, and backgrounds. Nobody will ever convince me otherwise. Kids are no different than all of us. Every kid is unique in so many ways. That was the first lesson I learned – on day one. Years ago, I thought parenting determined a child's demeanor, personality, and attitude, and I figured parenting was to blame for anything that ever went right or wrong with a child. Five minutes after meeting my daughter I changed my mind. She was strong and independent, and she gave off a distinct, discernible energy that ran right through me. Before I even ever said a word to her, I could tell she had her own unique fiery personality, and all I wanted to do was not screw that up.

That's how I look at parenting, and that's how I wrote this book. I want to parent my kids the way I want... because nobody will ever know them like I do. Someday, they'll grow old enough to take their life's reins, but for now I have to lead them. It's a tricky balance because I want them to be who they are... forever, but I feel I need to teach them how to do that. Teaching a kid how to be themselves is, in effect, the art of parenting (in my opinion). Ask ten million people how to do that and you'll get ten million different answers. Some answers would sound so drastically different than what you personally think that you'd probably laugh. Some people would laugh at your answer. That's an essential concept –

knowing that you have a distinct and important vision of how to help your kid navigate life. I'm not here to tell you how to do that. That's the stuff you'll figure out as you go. What I'm here to tell you is this... don't feel badly if other people do things differently. You need to be just like your child. You need to be who *you* are when parenting your kid. Find what works best for you and do that. Hopefully I can help expedite the process.

You're probably wondering... what makes me so special that I can dole out the exact same unsolicited parenting advice I'm warning you to steer clear of? Stop wondering that. I'm not important and I won't claim to be. All I've done is go through something you are about to. Because of that fact, I can help prepare you for what's to come.

I will tell you a little bit about myself though. I am, at the time of this writing, 36 years old, and I have two daughters. If I round up a few months, my oldest is five-years-old and my youngest is three. Yeah... I'm in the thick of it. You'll see. But, I wouldn't have it any other way. Also, I don't have any special certifications regarding child development. I am not a doctor, nor am I a psychology major or a teacher. What I am is unbiased. I work in finance and I like golf and fantasy football, and I enjoy writing. My education and training was spent in the trenches, parenting my kids every day since they were born. I'm here to pass along information... nothing more.

Oh, and I don't really like other people's kids. I don't dislike other people's kids necessarily, but I don't find other people's kids nearly as cute and amusing as their parents always seem to. You probably feel the same way, don't you? That won't make you a bad father – if you don't feel a natural gravitational pull toward all children. Kids on an airplane or in a movie theater annoy me just as much as they annoy you. It'll be different with your kid though and I can prove it. I'll just use my own kids as an example.

My girls are the cutest, most amusing people in the world. Everything they say is funny, witty, charming, and the exact opposite of annoying. I've never met anyone that didn't like my girls. In fact, they're both runway models in the making.

You don't care do you? Don't lie... I know you don't care. I wouldn't either if I were you. I actually believe what I said though. I truly believe my girls are the exception to the rule. If I'm raising the two ugliest, meanest, least charming children in human existence, I'd never know. In terms of your own kids, you'll wear the rose colored glasses too, so stop worrying and keep reading.

This book is for people like me, which is why it is short, sweet, extremely honest, and straight to the point. I have the attention span of a newborn gnat, and I couldn't handle 400 pages of rambling dissertation, so I assume you couldn't either. There are many scientifically-backed or research-focused parenting books on the market if you so desire, and many of them are great (I assume). But, if you're anything like me, you'd like to learn about being a dad in the easiest most efficient way possible. There's nothing wrong with that. Some people might call it lazy. I would call those people operationally inefficient.

To be honest, I actually never even picked up a book before becoming a dad. I still haven't. That's just who I am. I always just assumed I'd figure it all out on the fly. I did figure things out on the fly, and it's not rocket science, but a book like this would've helped me immensely. Believe me when I say it's a continual learning curve and not a day goes by where I don't learn something new. Use this book as a jumping off point. It will be a great resource for you. I know it'll be valuable because it would've been extremely helpful for me to have – mainly during those moments where I asked, "Is this normal?"

Worry

Let me ask you something. You're worried aren't you? I know you are. You're worried this book might not be good enough. You're worried you might not be good enough. And, you're worried your kid might not have enough advantages. You're worried about everything. Relax... your worry will never go away.

That doesn't make any sense does it? I just told you to stop worrying because you'll never stop worrying, right? That's right. Here's the first dirty little secret about parenting –

worry will never leave your side. That's actually the second lesson I ever learned, and the hardest. I still learn it every day. But, remember this; knowing and accepting the fact that you might worry about everything makes it easier. The awareness is the key. You won't want fear and concern hampering your parenting decisions (even though they probably will at times), but knowing they do affect your parenting decisions helps differentiate between good worry and bad worry.

Good worry is when you don't let your toddler cross the street without holding your hand. Bad worry is when you don't let your daughter date until she's thirty-nine. Good worry is protecting your child from harm before they know any better. Bad worry is when you let your own fears impact your child's ability to grow and evolve on their own.

Where do you draw the line you ask? Great question. Nobody knows exactly. People think they know but they don't. That's for you to decide. Welcome to parenthood. Just know this... worrying is normal. It means you care. In fact, worrying might be causing you to read this book in the first place. That's good worry, so don't worry. But, worrying about every little thing will drive you crazy because there's just too much you could worry about if you wanted. Bad worry is when you think yourself into feeling stress and anxiety. We all do it, but it's unnecessary.

For now, think about *where* the worry is coming from and *why* you're worried in the first place. My guess is your worry is based off one of two things: you're either worried you won't be a great father, or you're worried about your brand new baby growing up safely in the big, sometimes confusing world around us.

Both are legitimate concerns and I honestly still think about both from time to time. But, I know for certain, neither of those is worth worrying about. Much of where worrying originates from is the fear of the unknown. You're not sure if you possess the ability to be a great father because you've never been one before. Because of that fact, you're uncertain about your kid's future.

I believe once the path that lies in front of you becomes more visible, your anxiety will disappear (and excitement will take its place). So, let's dive right in and try to chisel away at the mountain of worries I know you've been piling up lately.

CHAPTER 2 – READY?

Let me start out by asking the one question that really matters.

Are you ready to be a great dad?

I'm guessing the majority of you who read this book and answer that question will say no. No is actually the right answer. And, it's the wrong answer. You probably viewed the question through a situational preparedness type of lens. You might have wondered about your house's setup, the baby's room, your knowledge base, or anything else you should accumulate between now and your baby's due date. On that end, whatever answer you gave was correct.

Whether you're ready or not, all of what you'll experience from here on out will be brand new, and the only way to truly become a great dad is, like anything else, through practice and experience. In that sense, you'll never be completely ready until you're a parent. Personally, I don't think it matters at all whether or not you feel ready to be a great dad.

If you want to be one, you will be. It's as simple as that. You might not believe me, but it really is that simple.

Nothing I've ever experienced compares to parenting. With sports, you can practice and get really good before the game is played. Subsequently, the games are easier to win. With work and school, studying can be just about all you need to succeed; the curriculum doesn't change much, rules are set in stone (or stored in books), and there are usually rigid boundaries available to guide us. Whether it's sports, school, work, or even buying a car, even though it's not always easy, the path to success is fairly straightforward.

Parenting is much more abstract. It's about effort and experience, understanding your own child, feeling their feelings with your own, following your intuition, and doing what you feel is right. A lot of people seem to be uncomfortable with playing things by feel. It's too unscientific for them. They want specific instructions on how to succeed. You can look online and find step by step guidelines to do practically anything. I'm telling you, it's just not like that with parenting. Anyone who says otherwise is simply stating their opinion as fact.

You can study all you want, babysitting your nieces and nephews doesn't hurt either, but conceptually... parenting is completely different than anything else. In my opinion, parenting is easier to be good at than almost anything else, even though it's one of the most difficult skills to master.

There's an instinctual nature to parenting. You already have natural abilities within you, genetically and evolutionary, that will surface at the right time to guide you when necessary. Trust your natural abilities as a human being. You weren't born knowing how to play hockey or how to drive a motorcycle, but somewhere deep inside you, tracing back thousands and thousands of years, you were born with an instinct to be a parent. Obviously you were born with the ability to conceive a child. Why would taking the next step be any different?

Plus, more than likely, you've had people in your life to guide you and parent you along the way. So, at least subconsciously, you've learned from them. If they were bad at parenting, you now know what not to do. Knowing what not to do is often times equally as important as knowing what to do. Conversely, if you were fortunate enough to have phenomenal parents or guides while you grew up, you can think back about all the things they did that made them great and follow their example. Most people probably have twenty or more years of good *and* bad experiences they can draw from. Use that knowledge. You already possess it.

If you didn't have many maternal or parental figures in your life, believe me when I say that's not going to hamper your ability to parent successfully. It might even help. If anything, you get to start with a cleaner slate than many others. No matter your background, we all started at the same place – not having the first damn clue what to do when we found out we had a baby on the way. The only thing I knew when I found out my fiancé was pregnant was that I wanted to be a great dad. I didn't know what that meant, but I knew I'd figure it out one way or another.

So, what constitutes success exactly? Again, that is a question only you can answer. That gets to the nature of what your goals are and how you want to parent your child. I will say one thing about the concept of being a successful parent though. If you *want* to be a great dad, you've already fought through 99% of the battle. Wanting to be a successful parent or guardian is the most important step toward becoming a great one. It goes without saying – the only reason I mention it is to quell your fears and worries. Again, if you're reading this book, there's enough inspiration and passion in your soul to seek self-improvement. It means you care. That you care enough to buy a book about becoming a great father is just about all you'll ever need. From here on out, you'll be accumulating extra credit.

The most important thing your kid will ever need is you and your presence. Even if you are living across the globe – just being involved as much as possible is the key. Your support, the touch of your hand against their cheek, being someone to lean on when they're frightened (even if you're just as frightened as they are), and your genuine love are what mean more to your child than anything I could ever convey. You don't need as much money as you probably think. You don't have to have life all figured out to teach them properly. Few people do. There's absolutely nothing you *have* to have in order to become a great dad aside from the fire inside you that burns desire. If you have that, you'll be great, end of story... even through your inevitable perceived failures. If you don't have that desire to be a great dad, nothing in this book will change that.

For all you soon-to-be dads whose wives or girlfriends bought them this book and are reading it out of obligation – relax, I know you still care. If you've gotten this far, the desire is probably there, even if you don't feel it very strongly quite yet. Take me for example. Seeing my daughter for the first time is what actually sparked the desire most intensely, so don't fret if you're not signing yourself up for baby classes just yet. I was dragged along to a few of those too, and I was bored the entire time. I'll repeat that. I was bored *the entire time!!* I pretended to be engaged, but I didn't learn anything through parenting classes. I learned by doing. I learned by seeing and touching and hearing and feeling. I learned the hard way many times. But, I had the desire to succeed, so I didn't let myself fail.

If you have the desire, you'll rise to the occasion when the time is right. That's the part that comes easy believe it or not. Think of it like building a house. Not metaphorically... just actually building a physical housing structure. Someone can give you the hammer, nails, wood, schematics, bulldozer, and whatever else, and you (like me) might stand there without a realistic idea of where to start. That's where I stood when I found out I was going to be a daddy, and that is probably where you are standing. Here's where the power comes from – even though you don't know how to build the house, if you live in Minnesota and winter is fast approaching, your survival instincts kick in and you figure it out pretty quickly. The easy part (and the most important) is to want to build the house. Needing to get it done is what inevitably gets it done. Believe me when I say, the rest will take care of itself.

Let's quickly cover one other topic before we dive into the mechanics of what to expect – the opinion of other people. I could write an entire book about this concept, but it would be a complete waste of time because that's exactly what other people's opinions are – a total waste of your time. You'll figure out pretty quickly what advice to take and what advice to slap right back at the person who gave it. Don't be afraid to ignore advice that doesn't feel right. Even throughout this book, please relate everything I say back to your personal situation and figure out how you want to do things yourself. I heard a thousand opinions about how breastfeeding a baby should be done and my first child only drank from a bottle. Everyone I know talked about how I should do everything I want to do in life before I had a kid because I wouldn't have time for myself once I became a dad. But even with two kids, I still find time to golf, write, hang out with friends, work, and watch football. I do everything I used to do (and more), and I have more responsibility than ever. In fact, I didn't even start writing until I had kids. If anything, my kids inspired me to do *more* than I ever have before. My brother has four kids, all under the age of seven, and he absolutely finds a way to live the life he wants to as well. Sure, your time management skills will be put to the test at times, but having a kid does *not* squash your dreams like people might say! Other people aren't you, so don't let them tell you what you're capable of. If they want to talk about what *they aren't* capable of, don't concern yourself with it.

Odds are high your priorities will change too, so anything you think you want right now could very well transition into something different ten months from now. If you play poker and drink beer every Saturday night right now, odds are high you'll still be able to do that for as long as you want to. But, eventually you might want to do something drastically different, and that's ok.

Everyone's situation is different. No two families and no two kids are exactly alike. Read this book in that frame of mind. Nothing I went through will be identical for you. Some things will probably be very similar. I'm trying to help build the skeleton of your house in that regard – so you can have a mental foundation of what's to come in the months and years that lie ahead. The more you know what to expect, the less anxious you'll find yourself. When I speak in absolutes, don't take my points as gospel, but just know that I'm merely expressing my experiences as more background for you to consider.

It's like art. The way I built my house may give you some ideas on how to build your own, but I'm sure your house will look completely different once it's been erected. Now, let's transition into the meat and potatoes section of the book.

I'll tell a quick story. I proposed to my fiancé about six years ago... give or take a few months. I don't even remember anymore. We were both in our early thirties so we decided to have kids right away – before marriage. Within two months we were pregnant. When she told me, I pretty much just froze up. I felt just like you're probably feeling right now. We went and played tennis, ate Vietnamese food, and watched a movie, and we both remained in a stunned trance the entire day. All I could think about was what having a kid would be like. I wondered if it would be a boy or a girl. I wondered if it would look like me, or if it would look like some random dude my fiancé worked with. I worried about being able to support a family on my own and I became *very* tense when I looked around the house and realized we weren't ready at all to welcome another member into our family. What I didn't think about were the nine months that stood between us and our due date. It didn't occur to me that the pregnancy was an actual phase of being a dad – the first phase. Pregnancy was actually one of the harder phases to go through (in hindsight).

Remember; don't spend too much time worrying about the future. Think about the now. Now is actually more important than anything else because now affects what happens in the future. I don't mean you should read 25 books and redecorate the entire house (your wife will probably take care of that), but I just mean you already have a baby. The baby can hear your voice. The baby can feel your touch. The baby understands your emotion and senses your mood. With everything you do, your baby will experience some version of it. I mention this fact because it's easy to forget it. You can't see the baby yet and obviously you can't hear it either. But, the baby feels you, and it's already developing a sense of the world it is about to come into. It is already learning, believe it or not. You are too.

CHAPTER 3 – PREGNANCY

Chances are high that this is the stage of the game in which you currently reside. Your girlfriend, wife, surrogate, fiancé, or someone you're adopting a baby from is pregnant. You're excited, nervous, and scared, and you've decided it's time to learn everything you can before the birth. Too late. There's not enough time to learn everything you need to know. It's not even worth trying.

I lied there. It'll feel exactly like that though – that there's not enough time to do everything you need to. I'll settle your nerves a bit by talking about how lazy I was during our pregnancy. I didn't do anything. I put the crib and some furniture together. That was about it. My fiancé bought a lot of baby toys and necessities, and her friends threw her a shower, so I had some leeway in being mostly useless. Honestly though, there's not all that much to do aside from enjoying everything. You'll probably want to get the baby's area ready. Whether it's a room, a corner in your room, or somewhere in the living room... put the furniture you have available together and get situated. In terms of absolute necessity, you don't need a whole lot else.

If you're a Type A personality and want to cover all your bases immediately, there are a lot more things you could potentially get: clothes, toys, a changing table, formula, a breast pump and all the accessories (if your wife will be pumping), bottles, nipples, swaddles, blankets, stuffed animals, diapers, baby wipes, teething instruments (rubber chew toys), booger suckers, books, stuff for bath time, a rocking chair, nightlight, baby monitor, a machine that plays music or white noise, car seat, stroller, high chair, and I could go on and on if I tried. There are lists you can find online that give you tons of ideas of things you'll need. Go crazy if you really want. You'll use everything I mentioned, depending on how your baby will eat. Just know that you'll likely get a lot of that stuff as gifts before the baby is born. Be strategic – I advise waiting until after the baby shower to get anything. The later in the pregnancy you wait to do any shopping the better. Give your friends and family ample time to stock your cabinets for you.

Baby proofing is a whole big exercise you'll go through where you cover light sockets, move dangerous objects, put the heavy TV out of reach, and basically de-humanize your entire house so your baby can't endanger itself in any way. We'll come back to baby proofing later on, but I'll say two things for now. First, plan on doing it... your baby will (eventually) find its way into anything and *EVERYTHING* it can get its hands on. Nothing is out of bounds to a baby or toddler. Second, relax. You have time. The baby won't be able to move at all for a few months. And, once it does start moving, it's a slow, excruciatingly frustrating process (for you and the baby). We'll get into all that later, but know that you have plenty of time to see what dangers lurk inside your house as your baby ages. I recommend doing it as you can. Whenever you see something (like a cord dangling from a lamp, cabinets that need locking, stove knobs that need removing), take care of it as you go about your days naturally. Before you know it, your house will have become a big square room with pads on the walls. That's pretty much the end goal.

Outside of getting things ready, I believe the main goal of the pregnancy should be to enjoy it as much as possible and try not to overthink. Snap some pictures. Take time to yourself and just relax whenever you get a chance. It should be a happy time for you. Specifically, whenever your wife is enjoying herself, kick your feet up and smile. The biggest difficulties you'll run into throughout the pregnancy will be to help your wife through her rough patches. My fiancé spent the entire fourth, fifth and sixth months of both of her pregnancies extremely sick. She was miserable. It turns out the term *morning sickness* doesn't actually mean how it reads. Morning sickness can last all day for months on end. Then toward the end of the pregnancy, my fiancé was very uncomfortable with how much the baby weighed and was ready to be done with it. Aside from those two phases, you should be able to relish the pregnancy phase fairly guilt-free.

It's exciting – watching the baby bump grow outward, starting to feel kicking and thumping, knowing you have a child on the way. I began to feel overprotective of my baby very early on. I started watching my fiancé's caffeine intake (she didn't drink much coffee, but she didn't appreciate the micromanagement at the same time), I would exercise with my fiancé to make sure she didn't fall down, and I'd try to cook foods that I thought would be best for baby to eat. Obviously, whatever your wife eats... baby eats, so assume you're feeding both at all times. I wouldn't let my fiancé stand on chairs to replace lightbulbs. We live in Minnesota, so I always wanted to be around when my fiancé walked outside during the winter months so I could help her navigate icy or slippery terrain. I found myself acting like a father before I felt I had officially become one. My instincts had kicked in and I didn't realize it. Looking back, I already was a father all throughout the pregnancy, but I was very scared to admit it.

With my first kid, I'll admit... I was scared for nine straight months. I shouldn't have been, but I was. I didn't want there to be any complications whatsoever. The thought of having an imperfect baby petrified me – to the point where I distanced myself (emotionally) from the baby the entire pregnancy. I didn't want to be devastated if the pregnancy turned into a miscarriage, or if the baby became physically or mentally disabled. Here's another dirty little secret. Everybody thinks about stuff like that but hardly anyone will admit to it. Everybody wants their perfect little baby to be born into a pile of white fluffy clouds just before scoring 10 on the Apgar test. It's normal to hope for perfection. It means you're emotionally invested.

That's bad worry though – thinking about situations you don't want to have happen. It's a waste of emotional energy. The testing is a joke too in my opinion. It eventually struck me as quite funny how the first thing our society does after a delivery is test our babies to see how perfect they are. Don't worry about that crap. Both my babies scored extremely high on the Apgar and we've endured challenges with both girls. I've known people who have had kids score low and turn into the most naturally gifted children I've ever seen. Forget about the testing.

Also, whenever you hear someone say something like, "As long as the baby is happy and healthy... ten fingers and ten toes... I'll be fine," they're really just passive aggressively saying they don't want their kid to have any physical, mental or emotional abnormalities at all. Don't judge them or yourself. It's normal to want your perfect baby. It doesn't make you a bad person to want everything to go just as you dreamt it. But I'm telling you right now, that's the wrong way to think. It's the wrong way to live. It's just one more thing to worry about. I'll share a few stories to help explain.

The ultrasound appointments with the gynecologist were an emotional train wreck for me. I was too nervous to function. At our 12 week appointment, where they can just start to hear the heartbeat for the first time (if the baby is positioned properly), I was terrified they wouldn't find a heartbeat. I felt sick to my stomach while I sat in the room and waited for the doctor. I found myself not wanting to be there at one point because I was driving myself crazy with fear. Eventually the doctor did emerge, found a heartbeat, and tears streamed down from my eyes as I listened to the echo of my daughter's thumping heart through the amplified speakers.

That was the moment everything became real for me. It is a moment I'll never forget. My child actually had a heartbeat. And to think, I'd almost ruined the whole moment by leaving too quickly. Even though I'd stayed, I didn't really enjoy it at all, except for the last few minutes.

I've known people who showed up to their 12 week appointment and the doctor never found a heartbeat. I have many friends who showed up and the doctor found two or three heartbeats. Imagine the shock when you listen for your one child's heartbeat, and you suddenly find out you have three children on the way! One of my friends found out they were having twins, and after a few months, one of the heartbeats stopped beating. There will be plenty of people who show up to their first ultrasound appointment and the doctor won't find a heartbeat, but only because the baby is improperly positioned in the woman's body.

Yeah... bad things can happen. It sucks. It's very rare, and worrying about it certainly doesn't help anything. One way or another, we find a way to endure. My friends who had miscarriages... they all went on to have kids after the fact. My friends who had one of their twins pass away while still inside momma were very sad, but the joy they felt when meeting their baby boy who survived was immense. There is still sweet in those unbelievably bitter moments.

I have friends and relatives who have kids with disabilities as well, and believe me when I say their love for their children is immeasurable. The fact that their kid was born with a disability didn't affect anyone's happiness... at all. They deal with challenges, sure, but not necessarily any more than the next person. The challenges they face every day are just different than other people's. And, in all my experience, the disabled child is absolutely no less happy than any other child in this world. The one thing you will care about most as a father is the level of your child's happiness. That is something I can just about guarantee you.

I'll tell you another story. My sister gave birth to a son about eight years ago, happy and healthy as the passive aggressive types will tell you, and she wanted a second kid a few years after that. She became pregnant again, went through the first 20 weeks without incident, and made her way to the "all-important" 20 week ultrasound (where the doctors can check development progression more thoroughly as well as check the sex of the baby). The doctors also check for growth patterns, movement, and various other indicators. The 20 week ultrasound was the moment my sister's life changed forever, but not how she initially thought it would. The doctors noticed her baby wasn't moving its arms and legs like it should. There were indications it may have one of a variety of physical or mental ailments, none of which were aligned with the perfect scenario my sister had no doubt dreamt up.

My sister was shattered. Her whole world was turned upside down in the blink of an eye. The doctors gave her the option to abort the pregnancy at that point because of how many "bad" things could happen. My sister didn't abort, and about four months later, she and her husband greeted her beautiful, perfect baby girl for the first time.

Her daughter was born with arthrogryposis, which is a condition that affects joint movement and muscle functionality. She has faced many challenges along the way. Now, my niece (who is almost five) is one of my inspirations in life. She's one of the happiest children I've ever met, and she has one of the strongest fighting mentalities I've ever known. After countless hours of physical therapy and many surgeries, she's now walking, dancing, laughing, playing, and living her life to the fullest. She has no idea people felt sorry for her and she doesn't care. My daughters have never even once asked about her legs or the casts she's worn most of her life – they don't care either. My sister... she's as happy as ever, and her daughter is still perfect. All the doctors who said my niece, who was also born with clubfeet, would never walk have already been proven wrong. Do you know who else was born with a clubfoot? I'll name a few people: Claudius (a Roman Emperor), Damon Wayans (the actor), Troy Aikman (yes, *that* Troy Aikman), Steven Gerard (a professional soccer player), and Kristi Yamaguchi (an Olympic figure skating gold medalist).

Your kid might not be perfect in the way that you dream it all up. They might not score 10 on the Apgar. They might not have green eyes or have curly hair, and they might not grow up to be a professional golfer. Perfect is a concept you're building up in your head beforehand. Once you meet your baby, you'll come to realize they actually are perfect. To you, they'll be perfect forever. Nothing will change that.

I don't talk about these things to scare you. I do it to illicit the exact opposite emotion. Your fear stems from yourself – from your own thoughts and expectations about what you think you want. Don't create fictitious scenarios in your head and worry about them coming true. Odds are, none of them will, and not in a negative way. None of what happened with my niece could have been predicted when my sister left her 20 week ultrasound appointment. Throughout my sister's dialogue with her doctors, and in all the follow-up appointments she endured, nobody even mentioned the word arthrogryposis. Some people who went through the exact same situation as my sister ended up giving birth to a baby with absolutely no disabilities at all.

My point is, don't waste these moments worrying about what types of struggles could emerge. You could find a million things to worry about if you tried hard enough. I absolutely regret wasting time wallowing in concern. At this point, I don't even remember what I hoped for when my fiancé was pregnant. All I know is... I want both of my daughters to be exactly as they are, and that will never change. To me, they are perfect, even with their imperfections. You and I aren't perfect... don't expect our children to be.

Enjoy your baby as it grows inside your wife. Touch your wife's belly throughout her entire pregnancy. Read stories to her belly at night when you're lying on the couch. Download the app that talks about what size fruit your baby compares to each week. I didn't do any of those things like I should have, and I don't have any memories to share because of it. It's ok to be excited, giddy and hopeful. Don't take away from the greatest moments you'll ever experience by fearing the moments that don't exist yet.

CHAPTER 4 – YOU

As your baby's delivery date draws nearer and nearer, my guess is you will find your thoughts focusing on yourself more and more. Can you do this? Are you strong enough to take care of a child? Will everything work out? What happens if you fail?

Know this – those thoughts are completely normal and natural. Self-doubt is a universal emotion. I believe everybody deals with varying degrees of self-doubt, whether they want to admit it or not. I admit it. I have absolutely no confidence in this book's ability to resonate with people. I'm aware that my ego is what's creating the self-doubt though, so I just try to battle through. As I mentioned before, you and I are both imperfect, but know that your mental and emotional fluctuations will have *zero* impact on your ability to be a great father.

My cousin gave me great advice one time (regarding writing). He said, "You'll have days where you'll feel like Shakespeare, and you'll have days where you'll feel like a dirty pile of hungover garbage, but your quality will just keep steadily going up." That should be your focus. You'll have piles of self-doubt at times, and your confidence will bounce all over the place, but the more you parent the better you'll get.

Oddly enough, one of the things I didn't worry about was my ability to rise to the occasion as a parent. I don't have a great reason for *why* I never doubted my parenting abilities, but I just didn't. I always leaned on the fact that I knew I *wanted* to be a great dad, and everything else would take care of itself. Believe me when I say, I'm no better than anyone else either. I could have worried a lot about my own deficiencies if I wanted (there are plenty to choose from). Just so you know I've indeed practiced what I'm preaching, I'll give you a short list of my deficiencies and situational challenges. You'll see – there's a lot I could have worried about if I chose to.

-I'm very shy, reserved and introverted
-I'm an empath and a very sensitive person, so I get affected very deeply by energies and emotional fluctuations
-I have a tough time making decisions
-I don't really like what I do for a living
-I've dealt with headaches as long as I can remember
-I've struggled with depression at various points in my life
-I've struggled with anxiety at various points in my life
-I've endured numerous panic attacks
-One doctor told me he thinks I'm Schizoaffective
-Another doctor told me he thinks I'm Bipolar

-I was diagnosed with Adjustment Disorder at one point
-Our condo is tiny and many of our neighbors do not like small children
-The people who live below us bang on our floor all the time (to get us to quiet our children)

Reading that list makes you uncomfortable doesn't it? I could list many more shortcomings, I'm sure of that, but I'll save myself the embarrassment.

Maybe some things on my list relate directly to you. Maybe you have a different list. Odds are, you have at least some weaknesses, and you might be wondering if any of them will affect your ability to parent. I'm sure you're wondering if any of the above bullet points affect my ability to parent successfully. It's a complicated question, but the simple answer is no... they don't. None of my parenting goals get derailed by my faults. My faults may affect how I parent in some ways, but not my ability to be successful.

I'll put it this way... nobody who knows me has ever said I'm not succeeding in the ways I want to be (as a father). They may think I should do things differently, but that's different. I'm caring and loving. I dote upon my daughters (probably too much), show them tons of affection, play with them, bathe them, feed them, stroke their hair while they fall asleep, and wake up with them every morning to get them ready for the day. I parent the way I believe is right. I am the person I want to be and they don't care about any of the aforementioned flaws. Your kid won't care about any of your flaws either. They'll want you to be there for them, hold them, and sing to them. When you smile and laugh with them, or when you give them a bath and wash their hair, even if they cry because they don't like their face getting wet, they'll look at you like you're Superman (or Batman if you're my oldest). You'll be their hero from the day they are born until the day you die. If you care enough to be a great father, you will be. That's the simple answer.

That said... everything your child goes through will affect how they see the world. So, who I am affects how they are and who they will become. The key is to look at everything from the child's perspective. What's best for them? Having a strong sense of awareness of how your child is affected by their surroundings is really the most important facet in judging yourself. The better you know yourself, the better you'll be at parenting your kid.

Personally, I'm always self-critiquing and adjusting my techniques accordingly. If I'm having a pissy day or if I feel sad about something, the first thing I'll do is admit it to myself. The more I recognize my own moods, the less it affects my kids. When my kids get scared after the angry guy below us pounds on our floor, I make a point of it to laugh it off. My girls respond to my reactions much more powerfully than they do to my explanations at this point in their lives. It bugs the hell out of me when I hear pounding on my floor, but I'd rather teach my girls to laugh than be angry, so I react accordingly. They see me laugh, and they laugh as well.

No, I probably will never be as stern a disciplinarian as my father was, but I find other ways to teach the lessons I need to teach. Yeah, I hope my girls don't develop bipolar disorder, or have to endure headaches their whole lives, but I'll teach them all about mental illness when they're old enough to understand. My situation is really no more challenging than anyone else's. It's just different. My brother works long hours and takes extended business trips, so he doesn't get to see his kids nearly as often as I see mine (and vice versa). My good friend is divorced, and my fiancé's best friend raises her kids as a single mother. Those two deal with a lot of challenges every single day of their lives. Their situations will never cause them to be an unsuccessful parent. Both of them care more about their children than anything else in this world. Their children will see the world differently than your kids might, but that doesn't make it right or wrong.

What's wrong is not caring. People will inevitably think you're instilling the "wrong" things into your kids, just because they don't agree with some specific aspect of your parenting, but not instilling anything at all is really what would be wrong.

Thinking about and critiquing yourself is just more proof you're on the right path right now. Don't ever let yourself think you won't be good enough. It's a paradox if you really think about it. You want to be good so badly that you end up convincing yourself you'll never be good enough. If and when you find yourself spiraling away in self-doubt, remember this...

You wouldn't be questioning yourself if you didn't care so much.

I'll get back to what I said earlier. If you care enough to think about the things you're thinking about right now, you're going to be a great father. You're already succeeding. The bad father is the one who is intentionally never around. He's the one who hits his kid, the person who tells his kid they'll never amount to anything, and the last person on earth who would ever be self-conscious enough to worry about being a great father. You're not him. You never will be. Keep trying to get better, but never worry about being good enough.

The important things you'll want to teach your kids are the things that are important to you personally. And if you let them, your kid will teach you a lot about life too – about how to be accepting, non-discriminatory and loving. Kids are unbelievable in the way they see the world. They have a lot of things figured out right from the get-go in terms of living life to the fullest and loving with all their hearts. What they need is your love in return. They need your love to be as unbiased as theirs. None of what you think you're lacking will ever affect your ability to love your child unconditionally.

When you get into wondering about how you'll teach your kid to defend against racism, engage in politics, or effectively debate global warming, you're just nitpicking. I've heard people say parents shouldn't cry in front of their kid, even if it's because they're actually really happy. I could argue that topic until I was blue in the face. I've never once, in 36 years to this date, bore witness to my dad crying. How is that any healthier? He was and still is a wonderful dad. How much crying is enough I would ask? Is there a point where it becomes too much? What types of things are acceptable to cry about? Is it ok to yell at your kid? How much yelling is too much? What if someone sets some other bad example in front of your kid? What should you say then? These are questions and discussions we could spend a lifetime on.

I'll say this... if you're dissecting your own ability to parent down to the above types of theoretical questions, you're going to be just fine. That's the fun part. You get to decide how you parent your kid. I have absolutely no doubt I'm instilling bad habits into my daughters somehow. You will too. Everyone is to some degree. I try as hard as I can, but I don't know how the world will operate in ten or twenty years. How can I possibly know how to perfectly prepare them for the future? I have strong opinions about a lot of things, but what if my opinions turn out to be wrong someday? Would it then be too late to re-train my daughters? It's too much to think about. The one concept I've settled on is to try to instill a strong work ethic in my girls and hope for the best.

I encourage you to not stress over decisions that won't be made until some point in the somewhat distant future. Think about anything and everything you want to and plan ahead for sure, but don't let the negativity take hold of you. All I would point out is that the answers you seek will all come from inside yourself at some point. Have faith in your own ability to overcome challenges and obstacles when they present themselves. I guarantee you, one day you'll look in the mirror and be awestruck at the inner strength you've continuously dug out. It's in your nature – to overcome. Call it evolution, call it natural selection, call it competitiveness, or call it whatever else, but it's in you and it helps you thrive. Have faith in your ability to thrive. Have faith in you and your child's resiliency.

CHAPTER 5 – BIRTH

The closer you get to your child's due date, the more energy you'll begin to feel all around. The anticipation will take hold, and your wife will be more eager to get that baby out of her than you could imagine. Every time your phone rings, a jolt of adrenaline will pierce through your body. You'll expect each call to be from your wife – telling you she's in labor. Time will pass more slowly throughout this process. You might feel yourself becoming more and more impatient as the days pass. Try to keep a calm mind. The day will come eventually, so don't worry about that.

Be prepared a month in advance. Even though it's more common to go past due with the first kid, some people do go early and that's not abnormal at all. Have a bag packed for a hospital stay and just be ready to go at the drop of a hat. Also, make sure to install your baby's car seat before your wife goes into labor. It's just easier to get it installed before you're at the hospital (dealing with everything else). You can get the installation inspected by your local fire department to make sure you've done it properly. It seems like a pain in the ass at first, but after installing it once or twice, you'll be able to move the entire seat between cars in less than a minute.

In terms of going into labor... one of two things will happen. Nature will take its course and your wife will go into labor, or enough time will pass where you'll end up having to schedule a cesarean section surgery. If your wife goes into a natural labor, it might not necessarily just come on instantaneously. She might dilate slowly – over the course of a few days or weeks – until her water breaks. Or, you might wake up in the middle of the night to messy sheets. One way or another, the baby will come into this world soon enough. It'll most likely look like a disheveled, scrunched up, sloppy mess, but you'll think you've just met an angel.

Don't expect anything to go a certain way. I could tell you a hundred different birth stories – all unique and all equally intense. Whatever happens, it will be intense. Try to eat some food before the delivery or you might feel light headed. I didn't faint but I've heard of it happening. Again, with the first kid, things have a tendency to drag out for quite a while, so you should have time to get to the hospital and take care of whatever you need to before anything pops out. You might even drive to the hospital once your wife goes into labor and get turned away because she hasn't progressed far enough to be admitted. You might eat a bunch – in preparation for a birth – and forget to eat again twelve hours later when the action really starts. It all depends. The likelihood of your wife getting stuck in an elevator and having an impromptu delivery moment is not high though, to say the least. Even though it happened with Zach Morris and Mr. Belding's wife, I can almost guarantee it won't happen to you.

When I say don't expect anything to go a certain way, I'm drawing on personal experience. I went through almost the entire spectrum of available options. In the end, both of my daughters were delivered by cesarean section, but I will elaborate.

My second daughter's surgery and delivery were flawless. Everything went smoother than I would have imagined. By that point I knew better than to imagine a smooth delivery though. At any rate, the surgeon went in and my daughter came out like a dream. There wasn't a single blip on the radar the entire time. Now, my first daughter's birth – that was in fact a complete fiasco. After a fairly uneventful pregnancy, relatively speaking, the due date came and went and we scheduled an inducement about a week into the future. We still hoped for a natural delivery, so the days just dragged by when nothing kept happening. Eager to meet our baby, we grew more and more restless as our day approached.

When our hospital check-in day finally arrived, I instantaneously didn't feel ready. I went from feeling excited to having tangible anxiety. We nervously got in the car, drove to the hospital, and settled into our room. The doctors immediately gave my fiancé a vaginal insert to induce her into labor and we waited a few hours.

Nothing happened. My anxiety turned into restlessness again pretty quickly.

We waited all night and into the next morning and still nothing happened. After about twelve hours, the doctors gave her a drug intravenously and we waited some more. Again, nothing significant happened. For the rest of the day and all night, my fiancé didn't dilate any further. I became extremely bored with everything and fell asleep on the room's couch at about two in the morning.

I awoke a few hours later to mass chaos. People were scrambling around the room. My fiancé was experiencing intense pain, which is obviously normal throughout labor, but she hadn't dilated enough to begin pushing. The doctors wouldn't let her eat so she was also extremely irritable. I was packed full of anxiety once again. Everyone in the room had become quite impatient by that point, so the doctors tried to speed things up even more. The surgeon gave my fiancé an epidural and manually broke her water.

Then, we waited some more.

Within maybe thirty minutes, the labor had intensified dramatically.

My fiancé had settled into her breathing exercises. She dilated further and further as the minutes passed. For as slowly as everything had progressed for nine months, I couldn't believe how intense everything had suddenly become. The whole situation was moving at the speed of light.

Then, it stopped... just like that. It literally felt like someone pressed pause and nothing moved an inch. My fiancé stopped dilating. All the energy in the room vanished. Even the catheter broke, and no urine was being drained from my fiancé's bladder anymore. So, we waited again.

The nurses replaced the catheter and nothing happened. They tried another one, but still no urine would drain. After a third failed attempt to remedy the catheter situation, a debate broke out about what to do next.

My fiancé and I waited patiently as all of the options were weighed.

They decided to go find our new surgeon and ask what they should do. The surgeon, who I'm fairly certain was younger than me, strode calmly into the room behind them when they returned. He asked us a few questions and right away I could tell he was too laid back for the situation.

I had had enough. Nobody could figure out how the hell to get my baby out of my fiancé, and now the new surgeon looked young enough to be attending elementary school. That was about the pace he moved at anyway – a sixth grader's. I didn't like him and I didn't like anything else going on.

"I think we should start surgery right away," he stated.

I immediately liked the kid. My fiancé and I agreed with his recommendation. I stuffed a few handfuls of peanuts into my face and gulped down about a gallon of water. The nurses proceeded to prep my fiancé for the surgery and they promptly wheeled her into the operating room. I dressed in the obligatory light blue garments and nervously wandered in behind them. I distinctly remember my only focus being on trying not to faint at that point. I sat down next to my fiancé and the cesarean section immediately began.

Fifteen minutes later, the surgeon pulled my baby girl out and I snapped a few pictures – pictures that would later reveal something incredible. For a full minute, nothing seemed abnormal. Nurses went to work on my new little sweetheart and the surgeon began closing up my fiancé's abdomen. I do remember wondering why my baby hadn't cried yet, but I wasn't concerned. I sat next to my fiancé while I watched the two nurses, who stood about fifteen feet away from me, poke around at my daughter near the back of the room. My daughter was positioned on a table that looked similar to a changing station with a scale on the top.

After the nondescript minute had passed, I noticed a nurse walk into the room. And then another nurse walked in. Red lights began flashing from the top of the table my baby had been placed on. More nurses came scrambling through the entryway. The surgeon's face looked calm, but I could tell he felt uneasy about what was happening behind him. The anesthesiologist standing beside me blushed with concern as well. He couldn't pull his eyes away from the mass of activity occurring near my daughter. There were so many people digging their hands around by my baby; I couldn't even see her through the wall of bodies. It was obvious something was really wrong.

I'm not joking when I say the scene was exactly the same ten minutes later. Ten whole minutes of that scene played out with no word as to what the hell was actually going on. I have time stamps on my camera to prove it. Finally at one point, a nurse walked over and my fiancé asked her if everything was going to be alright. The nurse sighed and said, "I can't promise anything. Your baby is just having a really tough time breathing right now. We're just trying to help her breathe a little better right now."

I almost fainted.

I thought it was a passive aggressive way to tell us our baby was slipping away and there was nothing they could do about it. When I looked past the nurse – back at the table where my baby was being worked on – I saw another nurse give someone across the room a thumbs up. I closed my eyes, shook the cobwebs away, and reopened them. The person across the room was now smiling back. And, that was it.

People started leaving. Someone brought our baby girl over to us and it was like nothing had ever happened. My fiancé and I officially met our new arrival while the nurses laughed and took pictures. Nobody seemed overly concerned about anything. I kept waiting for someone to finally unleash some bad news, but none came. The surgeon continued with finalizing the operation and the nurses brought our baby to the Newborn Intensive Care Unit for two hours of observation (even though they weren't worried about anything in particular). I just sort of wandered in circles for a while. I made my way into the NICU and stood next to my little sweetheart for a long time. I watched her wiggle her body, cry, look around the room with obvious confusion, and I felt her exuberant energy emanating outward. Eventually, the nurse explained to me how they just needed to jumpstart her breathing, and once they did, it was no big deal.

After my state of shock wore off and we got to bring our still unnamed sweetheart back to our room, we scanned through the handful of pictures I'd taken in the operating room. The most amazing picture in the bunch was of the surgeon holding up our girl just after he had yanked her out of my fiancé. I do mean yanked when I say that because the table my fiancé was lying on was literally wiggling around with how hard he had to pull around inside the uterus. In the picture, the surgeon's arms were outstretched, our baby was in his hands (covered in blood and slime), the umbilical cord hung down and drifted out of view below the bottom of the screen, and the nurse was staring directly at the cord. There, in the middle of the almost mythical looking umbilical cord, was a huge knot. Nobody had noticed it. Nobody really knew when it had formed. I assumed the nurse's head was already spinning by the time I took the picture. Sometimes I wish I could jump into that nurse's brain and listen-in to her thoughts right at the moment she noticed the knot. In that picture, her eyes were wide open, and I imagine she was a little anxious as she waited for picture time to be over and done with so she could deal with whatever was about to happen.

You're probably wondering why I told you that story right after I kept telling you not to worry about anything. I told the story for three reasons. First... it was an incredibly tense, crazy, rare, and surreal situation, and it still turned out to be no big deal in the end. Of all my friends, it is the most intense birth story I've heard. With doctors and nurses all around, the hospital is an amazingly supportive place and they can take care of a lot of different issues as they arise. I'm not suggesting you should not attempt a home delivery, which some people want, but only to assure you that the doctors and nurses know what they're doing. They deliver babies all the time, and they've pretty much seen it all.

Second... I mentioned how the catheter hadn't been functioning properly before the surgery, remember? Well, what ended up happening was when the surgeon opened up my fiancé, the first thing he noticed was a completely full bladder. It made him hurry his pace ever so slightly because he felt like there might be an issue. He told me afterward how seeing that right off the bat sent a shot of adrenaline through his system and, for a split second, he wondered if they should have spent more time trying to get the catheter to work beforehand. But after everything transpired the way it did with my daughter's breathing, he came to the following conclusion: the knot may have actually saved my daughter's life.

It probably formed when they were trying to induce my fiancé, and it also probably halted the attempted natural delivery at some point after that. Enough stuff had gotten twisted inside my fiancé to cut off their ability to drain the bladder, and when the nurses asked the surgeon about it he told them they should prep for surgery anyway. He told me that performing surgery on someone with a full bladder is very risky, and normally they'd spend more time making sure there weren't any issues with the bladder before beginning an operation. But, with how long everything had been dragging out up to that point, and because of how the labor stopped so abruptly, he had a strange feeling he needed to start the surgery right away. The human body is an amazing entity, and it knows how to signal for help in peculiar ways.

If we had tried a natural delivery, the knot may have become tighter and suffocated my daughter in the process. If the bladder hadn't stopped draining, the nurses wouldn't have notified the surgeon, and he wouldn't have expedited the operation. If my baby would have had to wait inside my fiancé while the nurses kept working to empty the bladder, or for any other reason, she may have completely suffocated. You'll be absolutely amazed at how the craziest chain of events will eventually lead to the perfect outcome. So, don't freak out about every little thing that happens. Every little thing that happens does actually happen for a reason.

The third reason I tell you all this is because it's my birth story and you'll have one too. Even if it's less dramatic, without anywhere near as much tension, and half as bizarre, you should still expect to go through an extremely intense situation that will stick with you forever. Your delivery room and your baby's birth will feel like a whirlwind you've never experienced. You'll be a hundred times more emotionally invested than any other doctor, nurse or relative in the delivery room, so everything that happens and every emotion you feel will be magnified to the size of the universe. I tell you all this so you know what to expect. Expect nothing in particular and, at the same time, expect anything can happen. But know in your heart of hearts it will work out for the best.

Kids are more resilient than you can imagine. They're built to survive. One friend of mine saw blood shoot across the room during her cesarean section. Another friend saw the doctor cut his wife's vagina with a scissors to allow more room for the baby to pass through after it had gotten stuck. Babies come out forward, backward, and upside down. Every birth story I've heard is different. Yours will be too. It's going to be a mess, so prepare your mind accordingly.

CHAPTER 6 – HOSPITAL

The hospital stay will be extremely draining. As with my case, the birth itself will take at least some toll on your emotional stability, but the aftermath is more of an actual drain. The reality of your newfound responsibilities will set in fairly quickly after you meet your perfect little angel, and the real difficulty lies in the fact that there will be no time for reprieve. At first, you might not notice anything because you'll be running on adrenaline the first night. You might invite friends and relatives to come meet the newest member of your family, and you will probably spend hours holding your sleeping little muffin, singing to it, talking to it, crying on it, and just flat out enjoying it. It really is a great time.

For some of you lucky ducks, you'll get to sneak in a nap and some food while your parents take turns loving on your new child. Take advantage of that time. Any free moment to yourself, do whatever it is you feel like doing. I recommend napping, even though you probably won't feel like it. Once everybody leaves and it's just you, the baby, and your wife, things will transition pretty quickly into real life. The only thing I'll advise (in terms of the first night) is don't let yourself fall asleep holding the baby. You'll be way more tired than you think and it's a very real risk to fall asleep on the couch with the baby on your belly. The baby can fall off or fall between you and the couch and get trapped without an avenue to breathe. Nurses will check on you quite often and there will be a bassinette in the room, so the likelihood of you pulling a real boneheaded maneuver right out of the gate is slim, but try to avoid the first night 'holding the baby nod-off' if possible. That said; do take a breather that first night. At that point, for me anyway, the worst part was over – the waiting. But, you should know that the most difficult part is just ahead. Rest up.

Now is a perfect time for me to sprinkle in another dirty little secret. I don't like babies. You might find yourself disliking babies pretty quickly too. I do like babies in the sense that they are beautiful, perfect, helpless, funny, amazing creatures, and I bet you'll already find yourself willing to lie in front of traffic to protect your baby from the minute it's born. That's not it. Babies are just irritating. They don't know what the hell they're doing. They don't know how to breastfeed right away (very well), they don't listen, they can't talk, they have no sense of danger at all, and worst of all... they cry. I'll say it again. They cry. And they cry. And, they cry. They cry about nothing. They cry about everything. You watch... for the first day or so, you'll think I'm wrong. You'll think your baby doesn't cry and only wants to sleep.

Don't fall for it. Your baby is tired at first... just like you. Your baby is tired from the entire pregnancy and also from the strenuous birth. It will absolutely *SNAP* to attention somewhere between that first night and second night. Your second night in the hospital will be the worst night of your life. I'm not even really trying to be overly dramatic. The second night in the hospital just sucks.

I'm giving you the most extreme picture here, but it's also the most likely picture. Your wife's milk will take a few days to fully come in and your baby will absolutely not care to have the patience to wait. I'll spare you all the gory details, but both my babies cried all night long that second night in the hospital. It's a very normal thing to have happen. Remember – babies are used to being awake at night and asleep during the day, and it takes a while for them to adjust once they get outside the uterus. So, just about the time you're hitting a physical and emotional brick wall by that second night, your baby will just be getting geared up for battle. It'll feel a lot like running out of gas just before the race officially begins.

The baby will still be on their schedule for at least a week or two, so when they spend all day sleeping, just know they might be up all night eating and playing. If you want to try to flip around your schedule before the baby is born, have at it. My fiancé did that with our second kid and it worked pretty well. Either way, one of the most important lessons to learn from this entire book is to absolutely NOT get caught off-guard by that second overnight in the hospital (and the schedule imbalance between you and your baby) because it can cause an extended ripple effect of negative consequences to occur.

We wanted to (and were able to) feed both our daughters breastmilk for roughly the first six months of their lives. That said, we went through bottles upon bottles of formula the second and third nights in the hospital with both girls, and even that wasn't enough to stop the unending shrieking. It just sucks, plain and simple. Take the little victories when you can. Nap when you can – usually, immediately after a feeding works best. Don't be a hero... you and your wife should trade off shifts.

Obviously, your wife will have to be doing the heavier lifting if she plans on breastfeeding predominantly, but both of you should take every second of sleep when you can get it. Leave the room too. Just taking a few minute break from the baby (and the crying) can revive your will exponentially, allowing you to dive back into the fight with renewed enthusiasm. If you find yourself getting frustrated, take a walk around the hospital and encourage your wife to do the same when she can. Neither of your senses of time will matter at all for a few days. You'll simply adhere to your baby's schedule and that's how life will be.

Don't use any of your own diapers, wipes, or formula while you stay at the hospital. Ask for theirs. They'll supply you with anything you need while you stay, so take advantage.

There's no sense paying for your own diapers while you're already paying for theirs while you stay. Use everything that you're already paying for. Also, there's a nursery available at many hospitals where you can send your baby for a few hours, and they'll take care of it while you sleep. Take advantage of that too. It's tough to send your brand new baby down the hall right away, but don't be afraid to. When we were in the hospital, most of the babies in the nursery were not their parents' first-born. It's so much easier to send your second or third kid down to the nursery. With your first, you'll have a tough time parting with it, even for a few minutes, but it's a valuable resource available to you that you can use. We used it and I'll never feel guilty about the two pristine hours of sleep it provided me. Those two hours of sleep rival any other consecutive two hour stretch of time in my life.

Moving on... there will be seemingly floods of people coming into your room throughout your entire stay. This is a time where you should be ready for opinions to come at you like water from a firehose. Your friends and family that come visit will have all the answers. That's to be expected. But expect much more than that. Lactation nurses will be by to show you how to breastfeed and help with the learning experience. This can be good and bad. It's good in the fact that they're extremely passionate about breastfeeding and will offer a lot of help, but the people we dealt with were bordering on pushy with their approach. To each their own, and obviously certain people are strong willed in their thoughts on breastfeeding versus formula feeding, but it might come off as overbearing to you (especially if you are impartial about how your baby feeds). With our first baby, it took a day and a half for us to realize that we were even allowed to ask for formula because the nurses seemed to want to push breastfeeding as much as they could. Just remember, it's your baby, and you can raise it however you want to. Take anyone else's advice as just that.

Doctors will come by to run routine tests. Nurses will do the same. Depending on the hospital, there will be photographers that come by to try to sell you family pictures. We had a pediatrician stop by to introduce himself (he ended up being our full-time pediatrician). The food service team called our room consistently to remind us to order our meals. Different representatives from various different child care and activity organizations stopped by to throw their two cents in about what our options would be down the road (regarding daily programs or activity centers our kids could attend). Some people even stopped by and I still don't know what their shtick was.

There will probably be a wide variety of visitors knocking on your door that you wouldn't expect. The main thing I would advise is to not be afraid to turn away anyone who you don't feel like hearing from. It can be really overwhelming – trying to learn the parenting basics while simultaneously holding off a storm surge of outside activity. If you're open to receiving all the information available, feel free to leave your door open to anyone who wants to visit with you. If not, don't feel badly about posting the 'Do Not Disturb' sign outside your door and only allowing entrance to those who absolutely need to be there.

After three or four days in the hospital, which will feel pretty surreal and timeless, you'll get booted out and will have to go home. I say 'have to go home' there because for me, it felt like I was being sent somewhere I didn't want to go yet. I wasn't ready to leave the hospital – where there was a continuous lifeline of nurses, doctors, food service offerings, and family members to latch onto whenever I felt like I'd hit a wall. It's a naked feeling being sent home. I felt a little overwhelmed – like I wasn't ready at all to start the parenting journey. I hadn't read any books like I mentioned, and the entire time in the hospital was spent trying to get my baby to stop crying and start eating. No routine had been set. Humans thrive on routine, and I was not thriving.

Expect that when you leave the hospital, you'll feel like a jumbled mess, and it's an uncomfortable and unsettling feeling to be honest. The good news is that things won't change once you get home. Your daily "routine" will be the same for a while in that there will be no routine quite yet (outside of feeding your baby and sleeping intermittently). In my experience, I found the best approach to be to live in the moment and accept that I might feel disoriented for a while. Just take things minute by minute and don't worry about anything else. Everybody's routine will slowly stabilize after a while.

Also, by the time you're leaving the hospital, your baby will have probably lost weight. Their weight decline might make you uncomfortable, considering how little weight they had to begin with, but that's all very normal and should be expected. Chances are, they'll continue to lose weight for about a week, but they should start to regain what they lost pretty quickly after that. Just as a side note, your child might potentially end up losing even more weight than the doctors would prefer. Both of my kids lost more weight than they were supposed to. It's typically not a big deal if your baby falls below their intended weight gain/loss threshold. As long as they've continued to improve their eating habits, their weight will normalize.

One thing I highly recommend is to do "skin-to-skin care" with your baby – both in the hospital and at home. It's exactly like how it sounds... you take your shirt off and let your naked baby lay on your chest for a while. The hospital staff will have your wife do it immediately after delivery, but it's important for the father to do skin-to-skin as well in my opinion. If nothing else (from your perspective), skin-to-skin is proven to promote bonding, and it reduces your baby's stress levels. Less stress equates to more sleep for the baby. Everybody wins.

Believe me when I say I could get into pages and pages of theory, backed by science, talking about the benefits of skin-to-skin. I could ramble on for hours about how molecules and energy waves can communicate and interact with each other in unimaginable ways. But, that's not my area of expertise, and I don't want you to think it's necessarily the *right* way to parent. I personally believe in it, and it's very easy to do, so if you care to learn more about the science behind skin-to-skin, please look into it more deeply. It's really fascinating and I do recommend using skin-to-skin care as much as possible.

The hospital can be a challenge, no doubt, but I have fond memories of the hospital stay (with both children). As time has passed, most of the difficult moments have evaporated from my memory, so a lot of what I remember about the hospital is the good stuff believe it or not. The good stuff comes easy, so I don't feel the need to prepare you too much for that. I'll mention a few good memories though... so you can see what you have to look forward to.

Holding my tiny little baby in my arm, with her body swaddled tightly like a little blanket football, is one of my favorite life memories. It's miraculous how something so perfect could come together so naturally. Feeling my baby's hand instinctively wrap itself around my finger might be one of the sweetest things I've ever felt. A baby's hand is like the size of a fifty cent piece and I remember staring at my daughter's hand for hours, marveling at its cuteness. Looking at my oldest daughter's face the first night I met her, my entire perspective on life changed pretty dramatically. I knew nothing would ever be the same. I wished I could spend every day with my daughter. I wished she would never grow old. It's a powerful feeling – meeting your child for the first time. It's a feeling I'll never let go of.

Like I mentioned before, I'm really not a big fan of babies (infants specifically), and until they are about three months old... it can be a real grind. As you're driving home from the hospital, probably doing about ten miles per hour, just know that every emotion you felt at the hospital is completely normal and any emotion you'll feel over the next few months is normal as well. The love, thankfulness, glee, irritation, agitation, and even the pure and unadulterated anger are emotions every parent goes through their whole life, let alone the first week of their first child's life.

It doesn't make you a bad parent if one day you think you might hate your baby. You might be overwhelmed quite a bit. Even if at some point early on you find yourself taking the really long way home from work or pretending you have somewhere to go after work (to delay getting home to the baby), just know that is completely normal. Your wife will do the same thing but she'll probably never admit to it. It's perfectly fine to want time away from your kid. It's healthy.

You may never feel overwhelmed either. I'm just personally a little sensitive to loud noises and crying, so babies – especially before they interact at a personal level – can wear on me. I think the intensity of the emotions you'll go through right away stems from the fact that it is all just brand new and you're not sure what to expect. With our second child, nothing we went through felt anywhere near as difficult as with our first (even though it really wasn't any easier). I think if I knew what to expect with our first daughter, I'd have had a lot easier time handling everything.

A lot of *"stuff"* gets thrown at you in a short amount of time right away. The birth and the hospital stay are especially emotional with your first kid. The learning curve can seem insurmountable. Remember this though... there's just a lot going on at that point. You'll pick it all up really quickly. Nobody I've personally known has ever said parenting was too hard. Maybe it still seems scary to you from where you're sitting right now, but every single person I've talked to ended up realizing it wasn't anywhere near as scary as they thought it would be. It's just different than they might have expected.

CHAPTER 7 – HOME

Getting home might be a really awkward feeling for you. This is where a lot of people snap out of their daze and realize they have no idea what to do next. You might get hit with an absolute flood of emotion once you get home. It might feel peaceful and chaotic at the exact same time. I remember feeling lost for a few hours. I didn't know which direction to start walking when I first opened the door. It seemed like I was sitting in purgatory – I wasn't sure what the next minute or hour would bring, and the feeling was extremely unnerving. I sat, staring at my baby, knowing she was depending on me for absolutely everything, and I didn't know anything at that point. I began to think maybe I had bitten off more than I could chew. Again, it's a normal feeling to have, but I thought maybe I was in over my head.

Then, the funniest thing happened. My daughter crapped in her pants. I know, right? That's not funny at all, is it? Nobody thinks that's funny. It's actually quite lame and formatively stupid. I'll never forget it though. To this day, even with a five-year-old and three-year-old still learning to potty train, I've never seen so much crap come out of someone's ass in my entire life. My baby at that time weighed somewhere near eight pounds and I was worried she lost half her weight into her diaper. Not just in her diaper, but everywhere else you could think. The poop covered every square inch of the inside and outside of her diaper, her bassinette and her blankets, and it went all the way up her back and across her shoulders. She had poop in her hair somehow. It wasn't like she sat in poop for an hour either. She crapped herself for at least ten consecutive seconds, which was funny, but we began changing her immediately afterward. It was like instantaneously... everywhere we looked there was poop. We had to give her two baths to clean it all off.

We'd been shoveling formula down her mouth (using a syringe) for three straight days and it must have all come out at once. The whole situation grounded me though. I knew what to do. Instinctively, I just did what anyone would do when a baby craps all over themselves. I cleaned it up. Then I fed her. Then, I burped her and held her again until she fell asleep. And after she woke up, I sang to her and talked to her while she stared at me and gave me strange looks. Even though babies can be really tough on occasion, they're actually really easy. They do like four things: eat, sleep, cry and poop. They only eat milk or formula for a good four to six months, they sleep like a cat (on an off all the time), and they only poop a few times a day. I'll let you figure out the poop stuff on your own – it's weird looking and changes with their dietary patterns, but it's almost too straightforward to dedicate much time to in this short book.

The tough part about the infant stage is that they need the constant attention and supervision. And, for the first month or so, they'll only sleep for an hour or two at a time before they get hungry. Let's talk about that next.

Feeding

Your baby will either drink breastmilk or formula for months on end. That's all they'll eat. Breastfeeding mechanics is an entire topic in its own right and one that I'm not going to cover extensively here. It's really hard for the woman though, I'll say that. The baby won't necessarily know exactly how to latch on at first, they'll want to feed constantly (and I mean *constantly*) for weeks on end, nipples will bleed, tears will be shed, and it all takes a pretty big toll. Some women I've spoken with say that breastfeeding is one of the toughest things they've ever done in their life. It's that hard.

That's why a lot of people use formula – breastfeeding is really, really hard to do consistently, and sometimes it just doesn't work, no matter how much you might want it to. Either way, starting out, the baby will want to feed every hour or two, play for an hour or two, and sleep for an hour or two. Every baby is different, but they run in pretty short intervals at first. The general concept is that over the first month, they'll slowly and progressively get a little better with the eating and sleeping until eventually they're eating more at each feeding and sleeping longer and longer. I'll tell a story about each of my daughters to give you a sense of the variability you might encounter.

My oldest didn't eat very well right away. She didn't breastfeed properly in the hospital and cried incessantly. We ended up feeding her formula through a syringe until my fiancé's milk came in. At home, she wanted to feed practically every half hour and would fall asleep on my fiancé's boob after having only ingested an ounce or less of milk. Typically, newborns drink between one and three ounces each feeding (with that amount increasing gradually as they age), so obviously that meant my daughter was undereating. For weeks, nothing changed. She wasn't gaining weight, my fiancé was still hurting (and sometimes bleeding) from her surgery, and something didn't quite feel right overall. So, we went to get things checked out.

It turned out the surgeon had accidentally left a piece of placenta inside my fiancé. With the entire fiasco that had ensued inside the operating room, he must have lost a bit of focus and didn't clean everything out properly. It was a very rare thing to have happen and apparently the piece of placenta still inside my fiancé was affecting the quality and taste of the milk she was producing. My fiancé went back in to have a D&C procedure (to clean the uterus properly) and within days, everything changed. Even though our baby girl had still not quite learned how to breastfeed straight from the nipple, her eating habits changed dramatically. My fiancé began pumping milk every few hours or so, and our baby would drink *massive* amounts of milk from a bottle. She gained a bunch of weight and everyone's sleeping patterns became more stable. No problemo.

With my youngest, we ran into an entirely different set of challenges. She was (and still is) much slighter than our oldest and seemed to have an acid reflux type of reaction when she ate too much. So, even though she did breastfeed, she didn't breastfeed quite like the experts wanted. She would latch onto the nipple and drink straight from the breast, but she'd only snack for a few minutes before dozing off – never really filling her stomach. As a result, she became addicted to my fiancé's boob (quite literally) and wouldn't take a bottle at all. She'd feed every hour, on the hour, and would refuse to leave her comfy lap spot in between feedings. We called her a tree froggy. She just clung to mama at all times. For months that cycle continued and she didn't gain weight like she should have (according to the weight charts doctors measure against). She was *much* more high-maintenance than our first baby, I'll put it that way.

For me, it was good and bad – with both. Our first only took a bottle, so that meant I was much more involved in the feeding process. Obviously my fiancé had to be the one pumping and supplying the milk, but I'd wake up in the early morning to prep the bottle and feed our little sweetheart. What was nice though was that she liked cold milk, so I didn't have to warm it up and go through that whole routine. It was more of a grind for me personally, waking up intermittently throughout the night, but I connected on a very deep emotional level with our oldest really quickly – much more so than with our youngest. With my oldest, she knew daddy from day one and we were pretty much inseparable from day one as a result.

My youngest didn't want anything to do with me for three or four months because I didn't have the milk. She wouldn't take a bottle from me (or anyone else) and we didn't develop a deep, intimate connection for a long time. It was really sad actually. No matter what I did or how hard I tried, she'd only let me hold her for a little while before she'd scream for her mama. There was good news though – I didn't get scheduled for any overnight shifts. Since I couldn't be of any use on the feeding side, there was no sense in me waking up to do anything. I got much more sleep with our second. I was working full time, so I didn't feel too guilty about it either. My fiancé didn't mind handling more of the overnights because she was able to nap during the day with both girls.

So in the end, feeding your baby will largely depend on their tendencies. I will reiterate though, there is a tradeoff. The more involved you are with feeding your baby at a young age, the tighter the bond you two will form immediately. Either way, it won't affect your long-term relationship, so don't worry about that. If your baby doesn't want anything to do with you for a few months or so, just be sure to take advantage of the extra sleep you'll be provided. You'll connect soon enough, but it can be hard to wait.

At about four to six-months-old, your baby will begin to eat real food. It'll be a slow transition, but you'll understand what to do by then. I would not even think about that at this point if I were you. If you're concerning yourself with your six-month-old's feeding habits while they're still inside your wife's belly, you're thinking entirely too much about it.

One of the biggest things to remind yourself of, regarding feeding a baby, is always burp the baby after they've finished. It's not a safety concern, but often times they will become extremely fussy after drinking just a few ounces of milk and you won't understand why they're so unsettled. Once you hear how loudly your baby can burp after feeding (especially from a bottle), you'll see why they were uncomfortable. They might not always cry if you don't burp them, but it is still good practice to get in the habit of immediately burping them nonetheless. That way you can avoid any fussiness before it ever starts, and you'll save yourself from more than a few headaches. Remember, the headache you never got feels just as good as the one you got rid of.

The mechanics of burping are pretty easy. Just set baby's stomach on your shoulder (so their head is barely hanging down toward your back) and pat their backside with the palm of your hand. Bounce yourself up and down a little bit and tap your hand all over their back until they burp. I would always start my tapping from the bottom of my daughter's back and work my way up toward her shoulders – it helped push the air out more efficiently. Whatever your method, spend at least a few minutes trying. Usually it won't even take that long. Sometimes it'll take a bit longer, but they should burp after almost every feeding. It's definitely worth the time invested. They might spit up a little bit with each burp, so if you don't want to ruin whatever shirt your wearing, have a towel or cloth laying on your shoulder just in case.

Sleeping

You'll hear it a lot. You'll hear it more than you care to. Sleep will be an issue for most of you. Sleep will likely be the biggest difficulty you'll face in terms of the immediate day to day adjustment you'll have to make. The few days in the hospital will probably be a blur because of how tired you'll be. Immediately after the birth, like I mentioned, you might get lulled into a false sense of security by your ability to find a few naps here and there. But once your baby snaps to attention, usually by about the second day or night, sleep will be hard to come by. The second night in the hospital will probably be the worst night of them all. I've mentioned that briefly. What makes the second night the worst is what makes the first month very difficult in general. It's a blatant slap across the face in terms of what your life will be like for a while. In general, you just won't sleep very much.

For me, it wasn't the lack of sleep that was taxing as much as it was the fact that I couldn't go to sleep when I wanted.

What I mean is this... I found myself as tired as I've ever been on numerous occasions, but the baby didn't care. There were moments where I desperately wanted just an hour or two to myself – to nap – but the baby wouldn't allow it. Not being able to sleep when you feel you absolutely have to will be a real mental barrier you'll have to overcome. If anyone reading this is a Marine or a Navy Seal, I'm sure you've done extensive training in this area. For anyone who hasn't mastered their functioning through sleep deprivation skills, I believe you'll find it to be tougher than you think.

The baby obviously needs constant supervision right away and you'll find him or her becoming angrily hungry at the worst possible time. The moment you lay your head down on the pillow, and I mean the exact millisecond you think you're drifting off to sleep, the baby will start screaming and demand another hour of attention. After that, it'll demand another hour. You'll get it fed again, changed, snuggled, and try to settle in for a quick nap. The baby will immediately demand more attention. You'll learn quickly that the baby determines your sleeping schedule infinitely more than you do.

You'll get desperate. You'll plead with God for one quick snooze. God will ignore you. No matter how badly you want to go to bed, you won't be able to until the baby decides it is ok. This in itself is tough enough. Where it inevitably leads is what I struggled with the most. In order to get your baby to sleep, you'll rock it and swaddle it and hold it on your belly or lay it next to you in your bed. Without even realizing it, you'll fall asleep. I guarantee you right now, almost universally; you will fall asleep with the baby on your lap or with the baby next to you on the couch (or in bed). That right there is a big no-no (according to almost every parenting book you'll ever read). That's what's called co-sleeping.

Co-sleeping is taboo in the world of parenting. Some people do it on accident and some people do it very intentionally. Having a baby sleep next to you increases the risk of SIDS (Sudden Infant Death Syndrome). A baby is quite helpless throughout the early stages of its life (close to a year on average). Sleeping next to a baby can increase the risk of suffocation – if you inadvertently roll onto it or if the baby smothers itself into your body or into a blanket (and can't move its head). I co-slept way more than I should have. It was an easy escape. I'd pull my baby doll right up next to me, feed her a bottle, and I wouldn't even try to stay awake sometimes. My fiancé did the same thing. It was always like using tobacco – I knew it was wrong but I couldn't stop doing it for the life of me. My guess is more people do it than will admit, but it definitely becomes a slippery slope once you start.

Each time I'd do it, I'd get more sleep than I otherwise would have, but I'd always wake up hating myself for taking the easy way out (and for potentially putting my baby in harm's way). What helped me was to remind myself what I was risking – my baby's safety and potentially its life. That was one situation where I did try to scare myself straight. Sometimes it worked and sometimes I'd still succumb to the evil pleasures of co-sleeping. Looking back, the one thing I would say is this; I know I shouldn't have done it at any point, but sometimes I couldn't help it. Do the best you can. Find what works for you. Sometimes I do wonder if co-sleeping is really worse than trying to parent without having slept at all. It sounds like a stupid question, but there were numerous times where I had to essentially choose between co-sleeping and being on the unsafe side of consciousness. Having only slept for a few hours over the course of a few days will cause its own set of issues to arise, so the choice is not always easy. The trouble I would get into is when I'd co-sleep when I didn't feel like I absolutely needed to. Don't be afraid to ask for help if you need it.

I cannot stress the phrase *"take turns"* enough throughout this book. Operationally, there's really no reason you and your wife can't both get necessary amounts of sleep throughout this learning process. At first, you probably won't get enough shuteye, mainly because it will all feel like such a chaotic cluster and you'll both find yourselves trying so hard to be good parents that you'll stay as involved as possible. You might even find yourself staying awake to audit your wife (or vice versa) – to make sure she doesn't fall asleep with the baby in her lap. If you both get at least a few hours of sleep here and there, you won't feel the need to audit. Once you have two kids, it can be nearly impossible at times to implement proper shifting techniques, so take advantage with your first kid.

When your wife is up, go to sleep. When she gets tired, and certainly tired enough to nod off while sitting upright, she should wake you up immediately. Then, you can take the baby for a while so your wife can sleep. I'm telling you right now; just two hours of uninterrupted sleep will feel like a month during those first few weeks, so manage your schedules accordingly. If you can find a pattern where you and your wife switch on and off, each alternating naps while the other takes the kid, you'll honestly get to a point where you'll think none of what I'm saying pertains at all to your situation. Sleep won't feel like an issue.

It's so important to perfect though – the sleep management side of parenting. In terms of all things safety-related, having one of you refreshed at all times (or as much as possible) will be among the most important things you could focus on while getting your feet under you.

CHAPTER 8 – SAFETY

I recommend brushing over this chapter a few times before your baby is born. You can also find a lot of free online resources to look through (that relate to baby safety). Even though some pointers in this chapter will be instinctual to you, this is the area in which I knew the least about before becoming a parent. Honestly, this is the only area I researched at all before my daughter was born. Even though some or all of this may come naturally to you, it's still good practice to review everything you can. None of what I'll talk about is difficult to grasp or implement. It just takes diligence. I figured it all out pretty quickly. You will too.

The safety of your baby is going to be important to you. That's like saying it's important to eat food and drink water. A lot of what you'll need to do will be done subconsciously as you care for your baby, but I'll mention what I think you should focus on the most. I'm sure your house is different than mine, so be on the lookout for anything I don't talk about that seems like it could pose a safety risk. For example, I don't have a garage at my condo so I'm not intimately familiar with what you might store in your garage that could harm a baby. I don't have a pool either... or a deck. Those are places I won't talk about that you'll definitely want to think about.

As you go about your day during the next several months, take periodic walks around your house and look at everything through the eyes of an overly-protective parent. Specific items to remove or defend against will become more and more obvious after your baby is born, so don't stress about being perfect right away. There's certainly going to be a safe learning period – where your kid moves around enough to teach you what to watch out for, but not so fast that you can't get ahead of it. You have plenty of time to work through everything you need to.

Your baby's crib should be completely empty for close to a year (while they sleep). The bedding should consist of a sheet, and that's about it. There shouldn't be soft bedding inside the crib. We would swaddle our baby and tuck in the top of the swaddle, so she had plenty of warmth around her, and we'd set her into the crib once she was already asleep. Form-fitted pajamas (I recommend the zipper footie style for ease) are ideal because they can act as a blanket for your baby while still providing a very safe sleeping environment. There shouldn't be any pillows or blankets lying around inside the crib while the baby is unsupervised. You should also avoid putting stuffed animals or other types of toys in with your baby at bedtime. Bumpers are not recommended either. Anything that could potentially suffocate your baby is obviously what needs to be avoided. Again, this is why co-sleeping can be so dangerous.

Don't leave your baby on anything that is raised off the ground (a couch, changing table, or bed) without your direct supervision. The changing table is likely the most risky because it is what you will probably use the most. Once your baby possesses the ability to squirm around and roll onto its side, you'll begin to understand why leaving it on a changing table can be so dangerous. Even if you turn your back for a second, your baby can worm off the side and fall down. The easiest trick in avoiding a changing table fall is to always keep it directly on the floor. No matter the age of your baby, if you keep your changing table grounded on the floor, they won't be able to fall off... it's as simple as that. If the table is permanently on the ground, you won't have to worry about them breaking loose. When they get a little older, they'll even gain strength enough to wrestle free from your grip while you're watching them directly, so I do recommend just keeping the changing table on the ground from day one.

Baby toys can pose a risk too. Usually baby toys are made to be safe, but be aware anyway. Babies sense a lot of things through the use of their hands and mouth. It won't be long until your baby wants to put anything and EVERYTHING into its mouth, and I do mean everything. Nothing will be off limits for them to grab and stuff in their mouth, so think long and hard about every little thing you give them and what else they could secure access to. It is safer to remove *access* to anything that might turn into a safety risk than it is to watch your kid play and take things away after the fact. Inevitably, they'll find something you never even thought they could get their hands on, but do your best. You can't be watching them 100% of the time for eighteen straight months, so get ahead of it.

Even at a very young age, you'll want your baby to squirm around by themselves. You'll encourage them to roll over, crawl, play, and explore at will, and the easiest approach is to only allow them access to anything safe. This gets back into baby proofing your house. By the time they become at all mobile, you should have had ample time to think through every little thing you have lying around (and gauge how necessary it is to have out). When you look around your house, think of everything you see as a toy because that's how your baby will see it. You can't even imagine the stuff they'll find a way to get into, so be on the safe side and just assume they'll get into anything you have out. This includes light sockets, food, cords, sharp objects and scissors, phones, pet toys, electronics, and paper products. Paper is dangerous because they will chew on it and soak it with their saliva, turning it into a soft, wet ball of choke-able hazard. Again, assume everything is a toy, and gauge how it would react to a baby's mouth. Once your child is walking, the entire game changes even more dramatically.

Check your house for landmines. Landmines are what I call things that can fall on your baby and injure them. TVs are a prime example of a landmine. They are typically heavy and can easily be pulled forward and off the stand (and onto a baby below). Once your baby becomes somewhat mobile, it will leverage tables to stand up against, and it will then grab hold of anything on top. TVs, lamps, computers, plates, glasses, and silverware are all prime candidates to get yanked on by your baby. You don't want anything like that falling from up above where your child is standing. Furniture (especially dressers) and appliances are also things you should look into strapping down so your baby can't climb on them and accidentally knock them over.

Check your house for sharp edges as well. Usually the corners of coffee tables and TV stands have sharp edging, which makes falling on them particularly painful. Again, once your baby grows into being a toddler, they'll use anything around them as leverage to stand up, and they'll fall ALL THE TIME. Try to make sure they can't fall onto anything sharp or dangerous. Sharp or jagged edges should either be removed completely or wrapped in soft material to make them less of a hazard.

Some other items to keep in mind... you should install safety locks on all doors and cabinets and put baby gates in areas you don't want your child to travel into. Be mindful of closing your toilet lids and emptying the bathtub after bath time. These are places your baby can get into eventually and they pose high safety risks. Try not to keep balloons around the house either. You'll probably get plenty while at the hospital, and they can be extremely choke-able if they become deflated. Cords (charging or otherwise) and curtains can pose a risk of strangulation to a baby. Watch out for anything hanging down toward the floor – the baby will want to grab on and can get itself caught. Stairs are of particular interest to most children once they start to become mobile, so either put gates around your stairs or always supervise your child while they're around stairs.

Most other baby safety measures are self-explanatory and you'll instinctively seek out safe ways to decorate around your child. Make sure your smoke detectors and fire alarms work properly. You'll know not to let your kid play near the fireplace when it's on, and it is common sense not to let a newborn chew on double-A batteries. The key things to keep in mind are: babies are weak and can get stuck places they can't get out of, they get into *absolutely everything,* and they will chew on *anything* they get their hands on. Anything lying around the house is something your baby will get into if you let them.

Miscellaneous Items

I'll restate it one more time because of how important I've found the concept to be. Taking regular breaks is actually a really good method in parenting. Sleep when you get a chance... you don't always know when or if you'll get your next chance.

With your first kid, especially throughout the first six months, you'll check on their breathing almost obsessively while they're sleeping. You won't be able to help it. You'll walk in the room, stand there motionless until you either hear them breathe or see their chest rise and fall, and then you'll sneak back out like you stole something. You'll learn right away, the old adage about never waking a sleeping baby is absolutely one of the truest bits of advice out there, but you'll risk it anyway – just to quadruple check your kid's breathing. You won't do it nearly as much with your second kid if you have one, but be prepared to harass the hell out of your first kid.

The first overnight, when your kid sleeps for six or eight hours consecutively, will scare the daylights out of you. Especially if you were sleeping at the same time and find yourself waking up to silence, you'll probably freak out and rush over to check the baby's pulse. It will just be such a sudden change compared to what's been happening that you'll get caught off-guard. This is an amazing moment in parenting though – it is the moment you realize your life won't be nearly as hectic as you thought it might be.

Giving your child a bath can be really fun, but it's a little unsettling as well, especially when they're brand new. Don't fill the tub very much (or just use a baby bath tub) and make sure the water is not too hot before plopping them in. When your baby gets wet, he or she will become extremely slippery, so don't hold them up in the air, and be careful when moving them around. Obviously, they should not be left unattended in the bath, but take extra caution even when you're present because a slippery squirmy baby can be like a wet bar of soap.

In general, a really good way to prepare for a baby is to bring one into your environment. If you have young nieces or nephews, invite them over for a few hours (before your baby is born) and follow them around your house. You'll learn almost instantaneously where you stand in the whole baby proofing process.

Your house will probably begin to look like a giant hand grenade as you think more about baby proofing. Again, I'm attacking this section like the parent who worries about everything, so it's really not as bad as it sounds. It doesn't make you a bad parent if your kid gets a hold of something you didn't want them to have. My kids perpetually found crap I never even knew we owned. It's unavoidable to make mistakes at times. The key is to learn from your mistakes. Take it day by day. Before you know it, you'll be ready for the chaos.

CHAPTER 9 – WIFE

know this is a book about parenting, but this is an important topic because it directly relates to raising a kid. First off, your wife is going to be put through quite a bit throughout this whole process. Physically, emotionally, and maybe even spiritually, she'll be put through the ringer. I can't speak to the science behind everything that happens during and after pregnancy (to a woman's body), but it is quite a LOT. Always be cognizant of that fact.

I'm not going to write too much about you needing to get your wife a push gift. Some men get their wife a gift for pushing out a baby. You can if you want. I didn't know that was a thing until well after the fact, so I didn't really get my fiancé anything. I've known people who have purchased their wife a diamond or a new car. And, one of my friends explained to me how he had given his wife the greatest gift of all – the gift of being able to carry his seed. He was joking, but I'm serious when I say she probably deserves extra attention and care. You will never have to go through the physical and chemical changes your wife will during this process, and you or I will never understand what that's like.

So, be mindful. Be mindful throughout the pregnancy. Your wife might feel worse than she lets on. There were times I thought my fiancé was a different person than I always knew... mainly because of the intensity of her mood swings. The changes your wife will go through will affect how she thinks, how she eats, how she feels, and what she wants, and you won't be able to relate to any of it really.

What I'm saying is... take care of her with an extra bit of diligence. She'll likely be judging herself more harshly than you're judging yourself. As fearful as you might be right now, she's probably even more scared. Chemicals and hormones within her body will just be all over the place, even well after the baby is born. I've dealt with mental health fluctuations myself, and they can be hard to battle through. Add in the physical toll your wife will go through, and it's challenging. Pregnancy can for sure trigger anxiety and depression in some women. When my fiancé spent three months of her pregnancy sick as can be, it took a toll on her state of mind. I think she felt as though she was missing out on something and was supposed to be enjoying her pregnancy more than she was. She felt guilty at times. Let your wife know it's ok if she hates being pregnant. Let her know it is ok for her to feel however she feels. To be blunt, there might be times where it's tough for you to say that, especially if you think she's overreacting to something, but say it anyway.

Some women love pregnancy and some women hate it, so your experience and your wife's will absolutely be different than my own. Just always be cognizant of how your wife's emotions are doing. Stress is one of the biggest catalysts for any type of illness, mental illness included, so be aware of how stress is affecting your wife's pregnancy. I'll be honest... it can be a *slippery* slope trying to work through certain patches of pregnancy. One time I made reference to our baby being stressed out by something and my fiancé took it as if I was pointing a finger at her – like she was stressing out the baby. That didn't go over very well. To the extent you can control it, try to provide a calm environment for you and your wife throughout the pregnancy. Any time you can eliminate external factors that might cause unnecessary strain, do it.

Your wife will be judging her own parenting pretty harshly after the baby is born. She's probably put a lot of pressure on herself as a mom already. There are a lot of things she might think she is 'supposed to be' or 'needs to feel' and they might be unrealistic. If the baby doesn't breastfeed perfectly, your wife might take it personally. If the baby cries a lot or if it doesn't calm down very easily, your wife might think she's not being a good mother. The themes in this book pertain to your wife as well. Convey to her that bad moms don't feel the need to judge their own parenting ability. The worse she feels about her parenting, the more evidence there is that she cares too much to be a bad mom. I'll never say anyone is a bad parent just because they don't judge their own parenting harshly. I'm only saying that people who are hard on themselves about parenting aren't the ones who need to be worried.

Passion leads to success more often than natural ability. Studies have proven that fact time and time again. Look into it if you don't believe me. Just think about it logically. Think of your favorite athlete. Better yet, think of the best athlete you've ever heard of. They're the one who spent the most time honing their craft. They're the person who works the hardest and cares the most. Tiger Woods didn't become the golfer he is because he was born that way. People think that because he was on TV at a really young age, but he has spent more time practicing golf than just about anyone in the world. Tom Brady is a workaholic and a perfectionist when it comes to football. Look at Michael Jordan, LeBron James, or Sidney Crosby. Look deep enough into any of those people's backgrounds and you'll find the person with the most intense fire burning deep down. My point isn't that you'll ever need to be those people or compare yourself to them. My point is that their passion is what eventually made them great. The passion inside you and your wife is what will sometimes make you feel inadequate. It means you care. It makes you great.

Because of what I'm talking about, be aware of postpartum depression. It can happen to you or your wife. It's a word you'll hear but you might not give it enough credence or its proper respect. Postpartum depression is a condition that can be debilitating. If you hear someone mention the phrase 'baby blues', they're really applying a less serious-sounding moniker to postpartum depression. If after your baby's birth, your wife's behavior seems drastically different than it had been, or if she seems unusually sad or lethargic, have a conversation about it. Don't be afraid to intervene if something seems off. Don't be embarrassed to admit something might be wrong. Talking openly about the difficult issues means you care.

Opinions

It might not be evident right away, but odds are high that you and your wife will differ on at least some parenting opinions. There are so many moments where you'll have to make decisions about what's best for your kid (both big and small decisions alike). Whether it's regarding an ideal bedtime or when to start feeding your little one real food, debates between you and your wife are sure to bubble up more and more as your child ages. It's probably not worth the effort to fight over what color hat your child should wear to the mall, but absolutely discuss big ticket items sooner than later (if you haven't already).

Things will change too. You can count on that. Before we had our first child, my fiancé refused to accept the fact that she could end up being a stay at home mom. She was actually quite certain she'd never be home full time with the kids. Now, she feels the complete opposite. She's home every day with both girls and wouldn't have it any other way.

Some of the discussions you've already had will take on a different tone at some point. Don't dig your heels in about things you might feel differently about a year from now. The world might look completely different to you once your kid is born (like it did with me), so sometimes it is best to defer certain discussions until later. Obviously, having a kid probably won't change your theory on what religion you want your kid to be raised within, but you might find yourself less concerned about other areas. For example, although we didn't really specifically discuss in great detail, my fiancé and I wanted to feed our daughter breastmilk and not use formula. After two straight days of listening to our baby cry, with neither of us having gotten more than a few hours' worth of sleep, our tune changed pretty quickly. Sometimes you might find yourself just taking what God gave you to work with and doing the best you can with it. Things change... just keep that in mind.

"There's more than one way to skin a cat," is a phrase to keep in mind for a few reasons. One... it's probably offensive at this point in time – to talk about a cat like that – which is why I used that specific phrase as an example. Your wife will do certain things that might offend you and vice versa. If she dresses your son in Winnie the Pooh outfits and prances him around a restaurant (that's sure to happen), you might lose your mind. That's right... all those other kids you saw running around with those stupid outfits on are about to become your kid. On the other end of the spectrum, when you bring the baby to a doctor's appointment and forget to put socks and a jacket on it, your wife might lose all faith in your ability to do anything. You're going to offend each other. Get used to it. You'll both find different ways to do the exact same thing. In the end, the kid got fed and went to the doctor, so it's not that big of a deal. Don't lose sight of the fact that you and your wife both have the same end goal in mind with your child. You both want your child to be safe and happy as they learn to grow into adulthood.

In terms of your relationship with your wife overall, there might be more strain put on it than there has been at any point you can remember. It's normal for a baby to affect a couple's relationship in many ways. It can go both ways actually. Having a kid can shine a light on a lot of differences you didn't realize you and your wife had, but it can also pull you closer together. And, it can do both at the exact same time. When we had our first child, for six or eight months, my fiancé and I worked great together as a team. Everything we did centered on our child and we never fought. But, the fact that everything we did centered on our child caught up with us eventually. We hadn't spent any time together in a long time and before we knew it, we sensed a distance between us we'd never felt before. For as much common ground as we stood on for those six or eight months, I couldn't believe the lack of intimacy we'd developed.

Get a babysitter and go on dates to stay connected. Go on a vacation without the baby. Do the things you always used to. Don't let having a kid derail the other parts of your life you've worked so hard to develop up to this point. Stay balanced. Let me repeat that one more time. Stay balanced.

CHAPTER 10 – TRICKS

'm no parenting deity, but I've picked up a few tricks of the trade along the way. I'll pass on what I've learned in a variety of areas. If I can save you some money or if I can prevent a few hours of confusion by inserting a couple useful weapons into your arsenal, I'll feel as though this section of the book will be worth its weight in gold. Nothing is meant to be a sales pitch, so don't feel like I am doing anything other than making personal suggestions. Some of these ideas might simply be stepping stones for new and improved processes you invent as you go. You'll probably notice that once you get the ball rolling (in terms of implementing some of these tricks), you'll churn out a ton of useful ideas. Hopefully I can get you started in the right spots.

Baby Gear

Start with the absolute bare essentials and work your way up as needed. Your natural instinct (and probably your wife's) will be to buy ten thousand baby-related items before the birth – just to be safe. Don't do it. You'll inevitably over-buy and you won't end up using 60% of it. You'll end up donating half the clothes you purchased because there aren't enough days in a year to fit them into your kid's wardrobe. Outside of the crib, car seat, clothes, and diapers, get only what you need and work up from there. Between the baby shower and hospital gifts, you'll be receiving quite a bit of stuff as you go. As I mentioned early on... give your friends and family every chance possible to stock your cabinets for you. Whatever your preference, be strategic in how you accumulate baby-related items. It's easy to massively overdo your spending. That said, I will talk through some specific items that have made my life as a parent much easier.

Toys

Your child will pick their toys like you pick your friends. They'll gravitate toward certain stuffed animals like it was made to be, and nothing will get in the way of your kid and their besties. This is good and bad. They'll develop a Lovie – a favorite blanket, book, stuffed animal, pacifier, or whatever else they can't live without – and it'll be your go-to item to calm them down whenever the waters get a little rough. That's the good. The bad is that if you ever lose said Lovie, the world will feel like it's about to collapse. So, whenever you sense your baby forming a tight bond with anything, get two or three more to keep as backups. My daughter fell in love with a blue blanket named Bee-bee and a brown stuffed animal (originally made for dogs) named Murphy. To this day, she doesn't go anywhere without one or the other. Before we knew any better, whenever either of them became misplaced, there was nothing we could do to calm down our sweetheart. One time, her original Murphy became torn apart and we made the mistake of sending him off to grandma's house for sewing surgery. My daughter immediately knew her best friend had vanished and the fact that we couldn't reunite her with her soulmate landed us in the doghouse pretty quickly. We definitely learned the hard way.

Now, we have about ten Murphy look-alikes stuffed somewhere in the back of our closet. My daughter saw them one time and got pretty confused, but I'd much rather have that conversation than deal with an unmanageable kid. Go buy another Bee-bee and Murphy and keep them stashed away for a rainy day. The avalanche of emotion that follows the destruction or misplacement of your baby's Lovie can be pretty heavy, so try to stay ahead of it.

Food and Snacks

Once your baby is old enough to eat real food (usually around six months), keep a bag of snacks and a bottle of water with you wherever you go. Babies and toddlers can become extremely fussy when they're hungry. In fact, their emotional state gets magnified to what'll feel like ten times a normal level whenever they're hungry, tired, restless, sad, or uncomfortable, so planning ahead is crucial. If you get caught away from home with a hungry child, there could be hell to pay. It can be easy to get carried away with the whole food and snacks concept – to the point where it takes an hour just to get ready to leave the house. I'm not saying you should go overboard by any means. Just keep your fridge stocked with simple, healthy, and efficient items so you can 'grab-and-go' each day. Some of the most effective items to carry along with you are: jars of baby food, sandwiches, bananas, string cheese, applesauce pouches, yogurt pouches, hard boiled eggs, and sliced fruit. I like to use a small hand held cooler to house snacks and water – so I can stock it up and store it in the fridge beforehand. Personally, I hate wasting time (or making things more difficult than they need to be in general), so I try to pre-plan accordingly. Do what works best for you, but always keeping a stash of nourishment within striking distance will absolutely save a lot of headache.

Bag

One key investment that I highly recommend is to get a baby bag (or travel bag). It can be any kind of bag or luggage tote... the concept is what matters. The bag should be small enough to be easily transportable, but large enough to handle the essentials: snacks as I just mentioned, diapers, wipes, extra clothes, toys, books, water, and anything else your baby has developed an affliction for. Some people pack a small plastic tote full of these items and keep it in their car permanently. Personally, I keep a box in my car with diapers, wipes, clothes, and a few toys, and I also keep a bag at the ready at all times. If I'm just taking the kids to the store or the coffee shop, I'll leave the bag at home (or just grab the mini-cooler). If I'll be taking the kids out and about for longer than an hour, I'll grab the mini-cooler with snacks, put it in my bag, and head out fully stocked. The idea regarding the car box, the snacks, and the handbag is to make everything measurably faster and easier. They should be pre-packed and readied as early as possible (potentially aside from making a sandwich or something) so you can take the kids wherever they need to go without wasting time preparing. And each time I come home afterward, I'll clean out any garbage or used diapers from the bag, immediately restock the items I used, and put the mini-cooler back in the fridge for later use. I try to keep everything perpetually locked and loaded not only because it allows me to get out of the house quickly and smoothly, but also because it helps me prepare other people to babysit my kids on short notice. Make it easy on yourself whenever possible.

Stroller or Carrier

The stroller or kid carrier is a must-have. Almost any parenting website or blog you read will have a section devoted to gear, and these two items are usually on top of the list (for good reason). A good stroller can be a Godsend. Obviously it serves the purpose of wheeling your little darling around town (without you having to carry them the whole time), but that's just the tip of the iceberg in terms of the benefits it will provide. It will have storage compartments and baskets for you to haul around the above and aforementioned necessities, so depending on the stroller or carrier you purchase, it can double as your baby bag too. Many strollers also have cup holders for your coffee (a must).

You can get a carabiner hook to clip to the stroller handle (to help cart any other hand-held items you'd want with you on your travels), and the stroller also provides an easy/efficient napping location for your baby (for when you're on the move). I recommend getting a stroller with a tray for putting food on. We use our stroller as a mobile feeding station all the time. I've used strollers without food trays and they drive me crazy.

A kid carrier provides the same amount of functionality, only you wear it like a backpack and your kid rides along. Some kids prefer a carrier over a stroller because they can keep an eye on mom or dad the entire time. For about a year and a half, my oldest daughter didn't like facing forward in her stroller because she'd lose sight of me. She loved the carrier because of her physical positioning, and she had fun riding in it as well. A good kid carrier gives you all the perks of a nicely made backpack, but it's also more compact and economical than a stroller is. Kid carriers are especially nice for those of you whose kid prefers to be held. You might want to wait on the carrier, but I'm fairly certain you'll want a stroller from day one.

Pajamas

Don't ever say I didn't advise you to only buy footie pajamas with a zipper up the front (or side). I don't even know why they make anything else. There is absolutely NO reason to put your kid to bed with anything that has buttons on it. From a pajama perspective, you need to think of everything in terms of how to change a diaper in the middle of the night (without waking your child) and adjust accordingly from there. Pajamas are as much for parents as they are for the kids. Don't forget that.

Realistically, odds are high you would never actually try to change your sleeping child's diaper, but the point remains – keep things as operationally efficient as possible. You will absolutely be changing diapers in the middle of the night, and you'll want to get it over with as soon as humanly possible. I also advise utilizing the night gown style pajamas (which have an open bottom with no zipper or buttons). Gowns are not suitable for infants, but they are amazingly efficient and comfortable for toddlers.

Baby Fussies

I hope I'll save you from a few of the major headaches I endured at the beginning of my parenting tenure with this section. There are only a handful of things that make an infant really fussy: being hungry, tired, hot, cold, or generally uncomfortable. So, when your baby starts crying, just start crossing things off the list.

Try a thorough feeding first. This can mean different things for different babies, so I'm really just saying you should make sure you're confident your baby is not hungry. Also, make sure they have proper levels of clothing on and make sure their diaper is clean. My girls didn't care at all when they had a dirty diaper but some babies do care quite a bit. Try burping them. If that doesn't work, but the baby just ate, try burping them again. Babies are extremely sensitive to physical discomfort. If their tummy hurts at all, you'll have a fussy baby on your hands. Sometimes they just have to poop, so you'll have to wait that one out if that's the case.

If you've crossed everything off the list up to this point, the baby might just need a nap. Even at three years old, when my daughter starts crying for no reason, it means she's exhausted. If your baby is fed, comfortable, and well-rested, and they still won't stop crying, you can try a few other things: take their temperature (to see if they're sick), swaddle them and hold them tightly, or bounce them around on your knee. Babies can be overstimulated as well. Both of my daughters would become irritable if they were around too many people, too much noise, or excessive amounts of light flashing. TVs, phones, iPads, and computers can also stimulate a baby to beyond their comfort level, so be mindful of their surroundings.

A lot of babies cry incessantly around 7pm. There are various theories as to why this happens, but both of my babies (like clockwork) became extremely fussy around 7pm almost every day and wouldn't calm down very easily. They didn't seem hungry or overly tired either. They just cried for a while. This can happen until they are a year old with some babies, and it can be very overwhelming.

You'll get to know your own baby pretty quickly and you'll find some tricks that help calm them down. The 'witching hour' as some people call it can be mitigated by simply giving your baby extra attention. Holding it, singing to it, bouncing it straight up and down, putting it in a holder or carrier and going for a walk – these are all measures I've found to be extremely useful in soothing a crying baby during its fussier moments.

White noise is also unbelievably effective. Apparently, babies hear specific sounds while they are growing inside mama's belly, and they become mesmerized by those same sounds even after birth. We have a music machine that plays the sound of a continuous heartbeat – a sound a baby essentially hears for nine straight months during the pregnancy. With our first child, we kept the heartbeat sound rolling for 24 hours a day until she turned three. She definitely responded to the heartbeat very well. Another effective white noise sound is just wind or air blowing. Apparently, the sound of blowing air (or 'whooshing' liquids) mimics the sound a baby becomes used to hearing inside mama's belly as well, and it worked very well to calm down our younger daughter during her first few months. Either way, just know that if your baby always seems to get riled up right around 7pm, and you can never seem to figure out a distinct cause, it's not unusual.

Your kid will get sick sometimes. The first time they get sick is concerning. You'll hate to see them struggle and you won't really know what to do. Inevitably, you'll show up to the doctor's office some day with a mostly healthy baby and the receptionist, nurse, and/or doctor will look at you like you're an idiot. If your baby isn't somewhat sick, they won't want to see it for very long. You'll feel shame and leave with your tail tucked between your legs. Don't feel dumb... it's really hard to tell if they're sick at first (especially with a newborn). And honestly, I still don't understand why doctors and nurses give the look of judgement since they should know by now that new parents freak out about everything. Either way, when you rush to the hospital for the first time after your kid gets the sniffles, and they turn you away with disgust, don't say I didn't warn you. It's a rite of passage in my opinion though. There are hotlines or nurse assistance lines to call with questions as well, and I highly recommend using those often.

After a few false alarms, it'll become pretty obvious to you if your baby needs to go to the doctor. Take them in if they become really lethargic or are running a significant temperature. Take them in if they won't stop crying and something seems wrong. As a caveat, I'll mention that I personally would not take them to the doctor unless crying has turned into a pattern and you've found no rhyme or reason for it. By that I mean if they cry for hours on end without pause, then go get an outside opinion. If your baby throws a fit every night around 7pm and is fine an hour or two later, that's not cause for concern. There can be other causes for a baby's crying that doctors can rectify, but it's not abnormal for a baby to cry for an hour or two without logical cause. In the end, use your judgment and gut feeling. I'm guessing you'll end up at intensive care when you don't need to be a few times right out of the gate, but you'll learn. It's better to err on the side of safety, so don't be afraid of overreacting. It's just more of a pain in the ass than anything else.

Teething

Before I had kids, I thought the teething phase would be a nightmare. It's really not bad at all. Your baby will begin teething fairly quickly – usually between three and six months old. At first, you'll think they've developed a cold. The onset of teething looks exactly like sickness. They'll have a runny nose, they might seem a bit congested, and their sleep will probably become more interrupted again. The first tooth seemed to be the most irritating to deal with for both of my girls. But, there are many remedies you can use to help alleviate their fussiness. Get some chew toys for them to gnaw on. Anything safe will work and they'll let you know their preference. Small rubber rings or animals always worked best for me. Ice cubes (large and non-choke-able), frozen washcloths, your finger, and wooden toys are also great for their chomping. I used to just rub my finger along my daughter's gum line when I knew she was teething and it really seemed to help her. Either way, your kid will just be a little fussier than they were leading up, so it should be fairly obvious to you when they start teething. Once they get that first tooth to poke through, which can take about a week or two (after the onset of fussiness), the rest aren't as bad. Compared to the first few weeks of their life, for me anyway, teething is a breeze.

CHAPTER 11 – YOUR BABY

As you read this book, you'll inevitably wonder about what else will go on with the baby on a day to day basis. It probably feels like I'm leaving a lot out. You might even be more worried now than when you started the book. All I've talked about so far are the things that cause headaches, right? Believe me... there's a method to my madness. If what you've read so far is the worst it can get, it can't be that bad right? It can be hard work, but it's fulfilling work. If you're passionate about being a great father, it won't feel much like work at all. It will feel like pursuing a passion, and the hard work will come easy. At any rate, I'd like to discuss the good stuff for a while... maybe talk you off the ledge a little bit.

Most of what I've discussed so far is universal. This chapter will get into more of the fun stuff – the stuff I've mainly left out until now. The topics I've avoided until this chapter are the moments between feeding and sleeping and crying – those are the times for you to be you. The moments I've left out are where you get to parent in that gray area where there's not always a right or wrong answer – where people will have a million different opinions about what you should do. Anywhere in this book where you think there's a gap in time – a place I haven't explained something in as much detail as you'd like – is where you'll have no problem coming up with stuff to do with your child. I know your child will eat, sleep, play and cry, but I don't know *how* exactly. You'll figure out the how pretty quickly in those areas. The uniqueness of your baby will determine quite a bit about how you do things.

Infants will just lie in your lap and stare at you, so there's not much to think about there. Outside of crying, eating or pooping, I'm betting the first few months of your child's life will consist of you holding them, showing them off to your friends, and getting to know their little idiosyncrasies. You'll lay them on their belly for tummy time and let them wiggle around on occasion. That's when you'll really start to notice yourself pushing them and encouraging them to move forward in life. When your tiny baby is battling to lift its head, screaming at you for making it have to work so hard, you'll begin to see your emotional and parental impact on its life. You are teaching your baby how to become a man or woman, one moment at a time, and it starts with the simple act of encouraging it to lift its head off the ground for a few seconds. The next day, your baby will lift its head for a few more seconds. Then, it'll roll onto its side a few weeks after that. You'll find yourself literally cheering out loud as your child figures out how to roll from its stomach all the way onto its back. Every day will bring new adventures and new progress. Every hour of your life you'll probably see your baby do something new. Sometimes you might be taken aback by how quickly your kid can learn new things. You'll see it become frustrated for very specific reasons. Instead of crying, your baby will yell at you, very deliberately, for a variety of reasons. Instead of wondering why your baby is upset, you'll begin to decipher its subtle communications to you and react accordingly. Grunts and screams will sound like words and sentences. Nobody but you and your wife will understand what they're actually saying when they make weird sounds and you will help translate it to the world around you.

You'll take pride in understanding the nonsensical babbling you hear. When your child wrestles itself from its back to its stomach, then finds a way onto its back again, you might beam proudness right before you cry tears of joy. You and your child's confidence levels will grow in tandem with each passing milestone. You'll find yourself laughing at the most random events – like when your kid crawls after the vacuum and starts crying when they find a way to accidentally flip it on. The most simple, ordinary, nondescript moments you experience with your baby will be forever burned into your happiest of memories.

I remember when my younger daughter was about a month old; we'd lay her on her back and let her hang out from time to time. If anyone got too far away, she'd start barking and squawking in our direction until we came near. Without using anything resembling real words, she'd be demanding we keep her in attendance at all times. She absolutely hated not being in the mix. Whatever anyone was doing, she always kept an eye out for shenanigans. Those are the types of things you'll pick up on, smile at, and never forget. You'll wonder if it's possible to love your baby any more than you already do, and a day later, you'll figure out that your love will never stop growing. At some point, the scent of cold stale piss your baby's diaper gives off will smell like vanilla extract, and you'll wonder if you've lost your mind completely. Nothing is flawless in this world, but you'll soon know, down to the furthest depths of your soul, that everything your baby is and does will always be more perfect than your wildest dreams. Even the tough days will turn into fond memories once they pass by.

You'll want time away from your baby too but you might feel guilty about it. That's normal. I cheer for the Vikings, so I'll compare it to that. I love the Vikings and I'd never root for another team, but eventually I just get sick and tired of them. I can't deal with them anymore. I feel bad about it, but I need time away to feel sorry for myself for having to put up with their crap all the time. I always come crawling back though because they're my squad. That's like the infant phase. You'll feel like you're going crazy sometimes. But, and especially at the three or four-month-old mark, you'll look forward to every second you spend with your kid. I can't describe the emotions you'll feel when your baby actually starts to interact with you, smile at you, analyze your face, poke your cheek, and prefer you to hold it over anyone else. The first time they smile at you, your heart will melt. When they try to swallow their own fist, your heart might skip a beat. Strangers will ogle at your baby at the mall or the grocery store and you'll feel proud. I never thought I'd be the guy to bring my baby to work (to show my coworkers) until I became a dad. I did all the crap I never thought I would. For example, I never thought I'd utter the phrase, "Soft footies please," until I became the parent of a rowdy toddler. Don't judge me... you'll say it too soon enough.

I discussed sleeping before – in terms of safety and your own sleep patterns – but I want to mention something else here. One of my favorite memories of my oldest daughter's infancy was rocking her to sleep every night. It became one of our many routines – me holding her in my arms, rocking her back and forth, singing Twinkle Twinkle Little Star to her while she stared up at me with her big baby doe eyes. I'd sing to her for a long time, her gaze always glued straight to my face, and eventually she'd slowly drift away. Her blinks would become more and more deliberate with each passing second until she closed her eyes for good. I'd continue to hold her for a while even after she was unconscious, not wanting to let her go. That's something I still think about all the time. The whole scene mesmerized me almost as much as it did her. Putting my daughter to bed was something I'd look forward to all day sometimes. As much trouble as she'd give me in the evenings on occasion, I couldn't do without those perfect nights.

Once a baby turns three-months-old, you're pretty much home free. It's an especially easy time when you look back because they're not grown enough to walk around and get themselves into trouble, but they've started to show some independence at the same time. They're old enough to eat well and sleep for longer durations, and you can also play with them, engage them, talk to them, and watch them respond to you in really funny ways. Even though they won't speak actual words for a year or more, they seem to perfectly understand what you're saying by this point. They can entertain themselves with very little prompting, and you won't believe how fun it will be to just lie next to them and watch them be themselves. They'll be silly, quirky, curious little monkeys and you won't want to look away.

Their personality, which can sometimes be extremely evident even from day one, will bubble out more and more. Instead of finding longer routes home from work, you'll duck out earlier. Weekends will come and go too quickly for your liking. Time in general will pass faster than you could imagine. When my first daughter turned three-months-old, I started to catch myself thinking back on her life and wishing I could re-live an old phase. Even though I didn't particularly love the infant stage, I started to miss it anyway. My baby doll was growing up and there was nothing I could do about it.

Your parenting will move to a whole new level once your kid is more interactive. You'll think more deeply about your baby's movements, learning processes, and likes or dislikes. Small, sometimes practically imperceptible changes to your baby's daily patterns will become obvious. You might even get a little cocky at some point – when you begin to understand how well you know your child. You'll feel connected at a level that runs deeper than you can probably imagine right now. It's really a great feeling. And don't worry... it just keeps getting better.

I could recant a thousand stories – to reflect the thousand different scenarios and routines I built into my everyday parenting. It evolves on its own over time. It's not all doom and gloom... not by any means... but the fun and easy moments are ones that come naturally, so I don't feel the need to prepare you for those. Those moments happen infinitely more than the frustrating moments. I'll leave those moments up to your imagination for now. You have to experience it all firsthand to fully understand. I promise you'll love it.

Just know that if you are indeed spending time with your child when you can, you're doing the right thing. You won't need to take your kid to Disneyland every day for them to be happy. I take my daughters to the grocery store every weekend in the morning and they absolutely love it. They might as well be at Disneyland. My weeknights and weekends are always full of perfect interactions. Lately my daughters like to climb into bed with us in the morning, peel my eyes open, and ask if I'll come build a snowman with them (it's a line from a Disney movie). There is no better way to wake up than to have your kid crawl on you and start fidgeting with your ears and mouth. My girls' sweet, high-pitched little voices, babbling on incessantly about anything and everything, fill the air every single morning. I can't help but smile.

All my kids want to do is be around me and their mama. There's nothing in the world more endearing than that. Even if I have errands to run or cleaning to do, my kids tag along. Your kid will probably love helping you shop or doing your chores with you. They'll love being involved in your life. If they could, your child would probably want to come to work with you each day and help you make money. There's nothing that means more to them than your involvement, love, and affection. They're like a dog that eventually learns how to talk. You're the center of their universe for a long time.

Remember, you get to decide how your child spends their days. You and your wife determine how your kid will treat other people, which political party they'll cheer for, and how they'll show affection. Decisions will be yours to make for a long, long time. You and your wife get to write this part of the book – the most important part of the book in my opinion. You and your wife get to fill in the gaps. Your family will evolve in the direction you want it to.

Throughout the pregnancy, whenever you catch yourself worrying about the future and you can't help it, turn your thoughts toward what kind of child you want to raise. Think about what kind of example you want to set. Imagine yourself teaching your child about humanity. When you worry about anything, try to self-reflect instead. Your child's reality will come straight from you for a long time. The more you think about your own strengths and weaknesses, the better parent you'll be. That's about all you can control.

CHAPTER 12 –
STRUGGLES

Regardless of how high maintenance your baby is or isn't, you're sure to run into struggles along the way. It is inevitable. There are just so many different variables to life itself that something is bound to be difficult. I can't say if (or when) you'll run across any real significant difficulties, but I can talk about personal experience. In this chapter I'll talk a little bit about the struggles I've endured so far just so you can see a few examples. Again, my goal is not to scare you, but to show you that struggles are often much more frightening to think about than they are to actually deal with first-hand.

I mentioned the difficulty we had in feeding each of our little girls. Our oldest turned the corner pretty quickly, but our youngest didn't eat very well for over a year. Her difficulty turned into an ongoing struggle for us as a family. Since she wouldn't eat very much at a time, seemingly because a full stomach made her uncomfortable, she didn't gain weight in tandem with the universal weight charts. She started out in the 50th percentile (in terms of how much she weighed relative to her age versus the national average), but by the time she was three months old she fell off the charts completely. She gained weight about as easily as I lose it. None of her doctor's appointments went very well. As a result, my fiancé worried about her weight incessantly. The more tricks we tried, and the more milk we shoved in front of my daughter, the worse everything became.

Given the fact that her overall development didn't seem to be affected, I wasn't concerned, although I did keep a close eye on it. I mapped her weight gain myself using separate charts that were based on babies who only drank from the breast, and she trended perfectly fine on my documents. I knew she wasn't eating as much as other babies and I knew she wasn't at ideal weight, but she didn't display any wildly concerning signs to me outside of a number on a scale. Even when the doctors, judging her progress under an intense microscope, labeled her as 'failing to thrive', I didn't panic. The only thing that really ever helps a difficult situation is to keep a calm mind and think it through logically, so that's what I did.

Still... I wasn't sure what to do. My daughter's blood tests were fine. Her vitals were normal. Nothing outside of her eating and weight gain was concerning at all. Doctors didn't believe there were any significant underlying issues, but they debated putting my daughter in the hospital nonetheless (to get feeding tubes put in). I didn't want my daughter in the hospital, but I didn't want to keep her from getting the proper treatment either. On the one hand, I had evidence something wasn't quite right, and numerous medical professionals weren't satisfied with my daughter's growth. On the other hand, my gut told me to wait it out. I constantly wondered if my personal bias and blind hope were outweighing my logic on the matter. It was the first really big decision I ever had to make as a parent.

One day I just figured... nobody knows my daughter better than me and my fiancé, so we'll make the best judgment we can with the information we have available. So, we held off for a while and continued our feeding efforts. It just felt like the right thing to do. My fiancé and I argued about it fairly often and it was very stressful, but we always stuck to doing what we thought was best.

Long story short, my daughter turned out fine. She didn't go to the hospital, and it probably wouldn't have made too big a difference one way or the other, but it worked out. One lesson I did learn was not to spend a lot of time concerning myself with national averages or standard timelines. I realize doctors understand medicine infinitely better than I ever will, and they have a lot of experience dealing with things I never have. But on the other end of the spectrum, I know my child better than they could ever hope to. No two situations are identical and every kid is different. I have never perceived different to mean wrong. I'm not saying ignore a doctor's advice. I'm only saying don't discount your own intuition. There will be times where you feel torn, just like I was. You might not know what the right answer is. But when in doubt, always trust your instincts. They are messages from your soul. You'll find a way to endure. Your child will do the same.

Here is another example. Since my youngest was always on the very thin and wiry side, she had a really hard time pooping for a while. Babies poop fairly efficiently when they breastfeed. The milk is made (in many ways miraculously) to be easily digestible. That's one of the reasons babies eat so often. Once they start eating real food, their poop will change dramatically. When my youngest began eating real food, she became dehydrated and was constipated *all the time,* and it hurt for her to poop. I personally disliked the pooping struggle more than the weight gain concern because my daughter was much more physically affected by being constipated. I hated to see her in pain. I absolutely hated it.

Almost every time she pooped, she'd stand in front of me crying, balancing against my chest, while I squeezed her abdomen with my hands very gently. Sometimes it would take five or ten minutes to get her through it. She'd eventually work out a really hard poop, and I felt so badly for her for having to deal with pain. But, it didn't affect her happiness for very long. After she pooped, she'd immediately return to her happy go lucky ways and didn't seem to remember what had just happened.

Sure, it was a struggle for a while, but there is always a silver lining. Each time I helped her poop it strengthened our bond – one that had been delayed due to her always wanting to cling to her mama throughout the early stages of her life. She began to trust me very deeply and she knew she'd be able to depend on me for anything. I didn't enjoy watching her suffer, but I know for a fact it brought us closer.

Enduring hardships has a way of bringing people closer together. The more battles my family has gone through, the closer we have become. I have no doubt the same will be true for you. The more often you're there for your children to lean on when they need a helping hand, the more trust they will always have in you. Any amount of suffering you come across and work through will only make you a better father in the long run.

CHAPTER 13 – OBSERVATIONS

I want to shine a light on some other somewhat random observations that will make you a great father. These are more all-encompassing types of examples that you're likely to run into. As always, use what you think is important to you and discard anything that seems irrelevant.

First of all, nobody cares about your kid. Remember that. I say that lightheartedly, but it's true. You'll be laughing hysterically when your kid dumps juice on its head at Perkins and you'll always think the whole world believes your kid is the cutest thing they've ever seen. But remember... and this is important... nobody else cares. Everything your kid does will be 'the funniest thing ever' or 'social media worthy' and you won't understand why people aren't asking you for your kid's autograph. When you tell stories about your kid at work and nobody listens, don't be embarrassed. It's the same as how you don't care about their kid. You don't care about my kids either. Don't let the fact that nobody cares about your kids detract from feeling proud all the time though. Feeling that way means you're a great father. Wanting to brag about them to the point where people become annoyed with you – that makes you a great father.

A lot of dads want a son. If you catch yourself hoping for a boy, don't feel bad. That's a normal thought process. It doesn't mean you're a sexist pig. It's not something I really thought about too much... but looking back, I probably would have hand-picked at least one of my kids to be a boy if I could have at the time. I will say this; having two girls did absolutely nothing to my state of mind. I honestly don't even think about what gender my kids are. My daughters are so distinctly different from each other I don't even think of them as both being girls either. My oldest daughter is a wild child – a bull in a China shop most of the time. She loves to wrestle, play catch, and run around all day. She acts exactly like how you'd stereotype a boy to be. She also loves art, music, movies, dancing, and dressing up like a princess. If you bumped into us at the store, she'd talk your ear off for hours if you let her. All she'll ever be to me is my Baby Doll. My youngest is shy, reserved, sweet, generous, and more introverted than most. I love how she's exactly like me in a lot of ways, but I love how my oldest is completely different from me at the same time.

I don't wish I had a son. I never find myself wanting to try for another kid just so I can have a boy. I don't think about anything but how much I enjoy spending time with my girls. Like I said, I don't even really think of my girls as girls. I think of them as my kids. Once you have a kid, I doubt you'll care at all about what sex they are. Odds are you won't even notice after a while.

This next bit of advice is for when your kid grows up a little bit; always, always remember... kids are like parrots. They'll repeat *everything* you say, so be careful. They'll also do anything you do. And, they'll rat you out at the drop of a hat. If you give them a treat to bribe them, and ask them not to tell mama, they'll gobble that thing up and tell mama the whole story. If you talk about sex in front of your kid or tell them you have a wart on your hand, expect everyone you know to hear the whole story the next time you bring your kid around.

Neither of my daughters can keep a secret to save their life either. I made fun of my boss one time to my fiancé and my daughter heard. I didn't think much about it until the first time my daughter met my boss a few weeks later. The first thing she asked him was if he became mean because he's greedy. I had to throw my daughter under the bus right back to save face. You'll catch yourself blaming stuff on your kids all the time too. Your public farts will get pinned on your kids, your tardiness to any gathering you attend will surely get pinned on your kids, and any time you leave work early, it'll be hidden behind a kid-related issue. I can't tell you how many times I went golfing when my boss thought I had to stay home with a sick daughter.

It comes back to the fact that your kid will want to be exactly like you. You're their hero. You always will be their hero. Whatever you do, they'll *have* to copy you. I don't know if they feel the *need* to do everything they see their parent do or if it's somehow instinctual, but your kid will want to follow in your footsteps in every way possible. It's very flattering and cute as can be but be careful. It can get you into trouble if you don't watch out.

On a serious note... having kids can turn your life around. Being an adult is tough. Sometimes it's awesome, but other times it flat out sucks. The constant pressures of responsibility, enduring multiple successes and failures alike, watching bad things happen to good people – it takes a toll on all of us. Depending on your stage in existence, you may be feeling stagnant, or you may be seeking a spiritual revival. Kids have a magical way of pulling out the appreciation in all of us. Their simplistic approach to life is inspiring – that's the best way I could describe it.

Sometimes, all you need is a tiny little spark that will reignite the passion for life you've felt slipping away as you've aged. My kids provided that spark and then some. I remember being somewhat unsatisfied with myself before having my first daughter. I didn't think too much about it at the time. I just went about my days feeling fairly uninspired. I didn't know what I wanted to be or what I wanted to do in life, but I knew I wasn't content. I assumed I needed to achieve more than I had. I felt like I was failing somehow.

When my first daughter was on the way, I started to worry about my life's path. I felt I hadn't done enough to give my child the best opportunity to succeed on their own someday.

Seeing my daughter for the first time made me realize what's important. Happiness is what matters. My happiness, my wife's, and my daughters – that's what comes first. That's what comes above everything else. Every decision I make now is through the lens of what makes us all happy. Seeing my daughter for the first time made me realize I already had everything I need to accomplish whatever I want in life. My feeling unsatisfied didn't change at all when I became a father. What changed was my willingness to accept that my satisfaction always came from within. Seeing my daughter made me want to become a better person. I wasn't satisfied with myself, and that's when I began to change.

I knew I wanted to take care of my daughter and be the best dad I could be. I knew money wouldn't make me nearly as happy as pursuing my dreams would. I didn't write at all before becoming a dad. Now, I write every day. I used to care what people said about me. I used to worry a lot about what others thought about me too. Now, I worry about what I think of others. Not in a judgmental way, but in a compassionate way. Having kids made me realize that everybody has a yearning for happiness. Everybody has feelings, hopes, dreams, aspirations, and fears. Deep within every one of us, there's a kid who just wants to play, have fun, and be happy.

If you're feeling unsatisfied, or if you find yourself wanting more, know that those feelings are what will help make you a great father. Those feelings are what will drive you to change for the better. The first time I heard my daughter say to me, "I love you daddy," I thought I had died and gone to heaven. The world hasn't looked the same since. Having kids changed me dramatically. I have no doubt your kids will change you too.

CHAPTER 14 –
CHECKING IN

Hopefully by now you are feeling a little more comfortable with what's to come. I've found that even just understanding where the uncomfortable moments might come from helps calm the nerves and give peace of mind. I told you about how I used to get aggressively nervous before games... back when I played hockey. What I didn't mention was how once the game started, all my anxiety disappeared. Playing the game was the fun part. Looking forward to the games was what wreaked havoc on my nervous system. The concept is no different with parenting. Looking forward to having a baby is when it's easy to let yourself get wrapped up in overthinking. Once you actually have the baby, your thought pattern will change. You won't have time to sit and worry about everything you might encounter. All you'll do is work through each encounter as it comes. And the more you parent, the easier everything will seem. With more experience, you'll simply realize how great a father you actually are.

I know firsthand that it's not always easy to get control of a wandering mind. It's not realistic to just shut off your brain at will. Thinking about all the stages of parenting and the nuances of baby behavior can easily become overwhelming. If you find yourself caught up in anxiety over the next few months, try to dig into the source of those emotions. What specifically is making you anxious? Why are you worrying? Dig internally until you find the root cause of your fears. Even if just to yourself, admit to your insecurities. You should be able to determine if what's making you worry is controllable or not pretty quickly.

If you can control what's making you feel anxious, take action. If you feel like preparing more by baby proofing, reading, talking to other parents, or babysitting your friend's kids, do it. Absolutely do whatever makes you feel more comfortable. If you find the source of your fear to be imbedded in your thinking about the future, worrying about what might go wrong, wondering how good of a parent you'll be, or anything along those lines, I promise you'll be a great father. Those thoughts mean you want to succeed. You'll be able to control all those things you're wondering about soon enough. Just have faith in yourself. If you care enough to worry, you'll care more than enough to be great.

It might feel like there's a lot being thrown at you right now, but this is like studying. Studying sucks. Parenting will be a lot different than any test you've ever taken. You'll take things as they come. You'll learn as you go. No amount of studying could ever teach you what your kid will be like, what food they'll prefer, or which sport they'll fall in love with. You don't know what their first word will be or when they'll start talking. There's not a book on this planet that'll tell you how to love your kid the most. Nobody would be able to parent your kid any better than you. You already have the answers to the most important questions you'll have to face. You just don't know what the questions will be yet.

Experience is what'll help you the most. You're just getting a head start right now. Remember... I didn't read anything before my first day on the job and I figured things out pretty quickly. I'm nothing special. We already covered that. The one quality I would say I possess that has helped me the most is caring intimately about being an awesome father. That drive is what turns my bad days into great learning experiences. That passion is what I look toward when I find myself riddled with self-doubt. Before I had kids, I didn't understand that the passion inside me is all I ever needed in the first place.

The Chinese philosopher Lao Tzu once said, "If you are depressed, you are living in the past. If you are anxious, you are living in the future. If you are at peace, you are living in the present." Remember those words for the rest of your life. Any time you find yourself stressed or worried, remind yourself that you wouldn't feel that way if you didn't care. Caring is what will make you a great father. Making mistakes is part of the journey. Making mistakes will never make you a bad father unless you don't care enough to learn from them.

I've never even met you and I have a world of faith in you. You're way ahead of where I was back then. I can't wait for you to meet your baby. I wish I could hear all about it. I'd pretend to care, when you told me all the things about your kid that make you proud, but I would legitimately love seeing the passion written all over your face while you spoke. Your heart won't be able to hold all the love you're about to encounter. Thinking about you becoming a dad makes me smile.

In a year or two, you'll have your own book to write. You'll have countless stories in your head to bore your friends with. You're ready to be a great daddy. You always were.

"Sometimes the littlest things take up the most room in your heart."
-Winnie the Pooh

Thanks for reading! I'd love to hear your feedback. Please don't hesitate to reach out with any pressing questions or concerns either. I'm more than happy to respond to any readers who graciously take the time to reach out to me. jimmysmeaux@gmail.com

Printed in Great Britain
by Amazon

25744032R00074